# THE One & Only casseroles and stews Cookbook

NEW HOLLAND

# THE
# One & Only
# casseroles
# and stews
# Cookbook

*All the recipes you will ever need*

With a Foreword by
**Jenny Linford**

NEW
HOLLAND

First published by New Holland Publishers in 2012
London • Cape Town • Sydney • Auckland

www.newhollandpubishers.com

86 Edgware Road, London W2 2EA, United Kingdom

Wembley Square, Solan Road, Gardens, Cape Town 8001, South Africa

1/66 Gibbes Street, Chatswood, NSW 2067, Australia
www.newholland.com.au

218 Lake Road, Northcote, Auckland 0746, New Zealand

Created by
Pulp Media, Richmond, London

Project Editors: Emma Wildsmith and Helena Caldon
Art Director: Susi Martin
Illustrations: Kuo Kang Chen

Photography: Charlotte Tolhurst, Stockfood Ltd, Philip Wilkins: 60-61, 84-85, 128-129, 172-173, 194-195, Shutterstock.com: 1, 2, 6, 10,14, 17, 18, 223, 224-5, 233, 238-239.
Every effort has been made to credit photographers and copyright-holders. If any have been overlooked we will be pleased to make the necessary corrections in subsequent editions.

Publisher: James Tavendale
www.pulp.me.uk

A record of this book is available from the National Library.
ISBN 9781742572437
Printed in Italy
10 9 8 7 6 5 4 3 2 1

"A good casserole is like a good marriage: only those responsible for it really know what goes in it."

anonymous

# Contents

# Foreword

## By Jenny Linford

When it comes to comfort food, one-pot dishes such as casseroles and stews score very highly. There is something very satisfying about the transformative process which sees an assortment of ingredients – such as cheap cuts of meat and everyday vegetables – metamorphosis through a long, slow, cheek-by-jowl cooking process into a wonderfully flavourful, unified dish. Similarly, oven-baked dishes – such as gratins – meld together different ingredients during the cooking process to create a deliciously hearty end result.

### The importance of browning

Many stews often start with a preliminary frying stage, a start of
the cooking process which allows ingredients to give off flavour
and soften. When it comes to cooking meat or poultry, this stage is
particularly important as browning the meat creates a rich, savoury
flavour. For successful browning, ensure that you thoroughly preheat
the fat before adding in the meat or poultry.

### Go slow

The key to successfully creating stews and casseroles is not to be
in a hurry. There are no short cuts; reducing the cooking time will
simply result in tough meat and a dish that seriously lacks flavour.
Slow should mean slow. What's required is very gentle simmering on
the hob or cooking in a low oven. The joy about this sort of cooking
is that once everything is in the pot it can simply be left alone to cook
unattended for 2–3 hours. Investing in a good quality heavy casserole
dish is well worth the money as it will conduct the heat efficiently
while lessening the risk of scorching or burning.

### Thrifty cooking

Satisfyingly, many of the cuts of meat or poultry that are the best
for stews and casseroles are also the cheapest. Cuts such as lamb
shanks, beef cheeks, chicken thighs – that is cuts of meat on the
bone or with a high fat content – are those which produce the tastiest

result. As a general rule of thumb, cuts that lend themselves to quick cooking, such as chicken breast fillets or fillet steaks, are not what you want when making a stew. Similarly, affordable staples, such as root vegetables or pulses, lend themselves to slow cooking in this way.

### Make in advance

The secret to a really flavourful stew or casserole is very simple: cook it a day or two **ahead of time**. Once cooked, set it aside to cool, then chill until required, heating through thoroughly before serving. This setting aside process allows the flavours to develop and mature. It makes stews and casseroles the perfect choice when it comes to entertaining as it allows the bulk of the cooking to be done in advance. Another advantage of making a stew then cooling and chilling it, is that any fat in the dish will set and form a layer on top, which can then be easily skimmed off, cutting down on the fat content.

### Creating flavour

When cooking with stock, one way to intensify its flavour is to reduce it through rapid boiling before adding it to the dish. Similarly, wine, beer or cider are often used as a liquid base for casseroles gain in intensity through partial reduction. Adding fresh or dried herbs, fragrant spices, dried fruits or strong tasting ingredients such as wild mushrooms or garlic sausage are all simple but effective ways of boosting flavour.

### Great gratins

When it comes to root vegetable gratins, such as classic potato gratin, the best way to ensure that the vegetables will be sufficiently cooked through is to blanch the sliced vegetables briefly in boiling water before layering in the gratin dish.

Once you've mastered the basic principles of how to make a gratin, then numerous variations are possible. Your chosen cooking liquid can vary from dairy-based ones such a mild, milk-based white sauce or rich double cream to tasty chicken, meat, fish or vegetable stock. One simple way to tweak gratins is to combine ingredients. For example, mixing celeriac or sweet potatoes or Jerusalem artichokes with potatoes produces very differently flavoured results from a straight potato gratin.

Gratins and oven bakes benefit from the textural contrast between a crisp topping and a 'soft' interior. With that in mind, be generous with your chosen topping, sprinkling it evenly so that it forms a protective layer over the dish. Classic gratin toppings include grated hard cheese, such as Parmesan or Cheddar, which melt well. For a crunchy effect, mix in fresh or dried breadcrumbs, seeds or chopped nuts.

# Bacon, butternut, pearl barley and leek stew

**1.** Melt 25g of butter and oil together in a large pan. Fry the pork for 5 minutes, until golden brown. Stir in the leeks and garlic, and cook for 2 minutes.

**2.** Add the barley, squash, carrots, thyme, sage, stock and seasoning. Bring to the boil, cover and simmer for 25 minutes until the barley is just tender.

**3.** Meanwhile, using your fingertips, rub together the flour, remaining butter and cheese until the mixture resembles breadcrumbs. Stir in the parsley, seasoning and enough water to form a soft dough. Divide into walnut-size pieces and roll into balls. Add these to the stew and cook for another 20 minutes, until the dumplings are cooked. Scatter some thyme over the stew to garnish.

Preparation time: 25 min
Cooking time: 1 h 5 min
Serves 4

100g butter
1 tbsp olive oil
400g pork belly, cut into 2cm pieces
2 leeks, thickly sliced
2 garlic cloves, crushed
250g pearl barley
250g butternut squash, peeled and
    cut into cubes
200g Chantenay carrots, trimmed
2 tbsp fresh chopped thyme
1 tbsp fresh chopped sage
1.15l good chicken stock
175g self-raising flour
100g Stilton, grated
2 tbsp fresh chopped parsley
salt and pepper to season
fresh thyme to garnish

# Celeriac, fennel and bean stew

**1.** Heat the oil in a large pan and cook the celery, fennel, celeriac and leeks for 5 minutes, stirring occasionally. Add the rosemary, garlic, beans, green beans and stock, and season. Bring to a boil. Cover and allow it to simmer for 10 minutes.

**2.** Stir in the cabbage and bring the stew to a boil. Allow it to simmer for another 5 minutes. Add shredded crusty bread and freshly grated Parmesan, and serve immediately.

Preparation time: 10 min
Cooking time: 20 min
Serves 4

*2 tbsp olive oil*
*1 celery heart, sliced*
*1 bulb of fennel, chopped*
*250g celeriac, peeled and cut into*
  *1cm pieces*
*2 leeks, sliced*
*1 tbsp fresh chopped rosemary*
*2 garlic cloves, chopped*
*1 x 410g can mixed beans, drained*
  *thoroughly*
*220g green beans, cut in half*
*800ml good vegetable stock*
*½ small Savoy cabbage,*
*shredded crusty bread and freshly*
  *grated Parmesan, to serve*

# Coq au Vin

**1.** Heat 3 tablespoons of oil in large frying pan and cook the bacon and shallots for 5 minutes, until golden. Remove from the pan using a slotted spoon and keep warm. Add the mushrooms and cook for 5 minutes, until golden. Remove from the pan.

**2.** Meanwhile season the flour and toss in the chicken pieces to coat evenly. Add the chicken to the pan and cook for 5 minutes, turning occasionally until golden.

**3.** Add the bacon and shallots to the pan with the brandy. Heat slightly and ignite, and leave until the flames have subsided. Stir in the red wine, bouquet garni, garlic and season. Bring to the boil and cover, and simmer for 50 minutes, until the chicken is tender.

**4.** Stir in the mushrooms and simmer for a further 10 minutes. Discard the bouquet garni and serve with new potatoes.

Preparation time: 15 min
Cooking time: 1 h 15 min
Serves 4

*5 tbsp olive oil*
*100g rashers smoked streaky bacon,*
  *cut into pieces*
*175g shallots*
*225g button chestnut mushrooms*
*1 tbsp plain flour*
*8 chicken thighs*
*2 tbsp brandy*
*300ml red wine*
*1 bouquet garni*
*2 garlic cloves, chopped*
*boiled new potatoes, to serve*

# Spicy sausage and bean stew with soured cream and guacamole

Preparation time: 15 min
Cooking time: 50 min
Serves 4

*For the stew:*
*2 tbsp olive oil*
*8 x good-quality sausages*
*1 red onion, cut into wedges*
*2 garlic cloves, chopped*
*2 tsp chilli powder*
*2 tsp mixed spice*
*2 tbsp paprika*
*2 x 400g cans chopped tomatoes*
*1 tbsp tomato puree*
*1 x 400g can chilli beans*
*1 x 415g baked beans*

*For the guacamole:*
*2 ripe avocadoes, stoned*
*4 spring onions, sliced diagonally*
*2 medium tomatoes, deseeded and*
  *chopped*
*2 tbsp fresh chopped coriander*
*1 x 150ml carton soured cream or*
  *crème fraîche*

1. For the stew, heat the oil in a casserole dish and cook the sausages for about 10 minutes, turning occasionally until golden. Remove from the pan and set aside.

2. Add the onion and garlic and cook for 5 minutes, until softened. Stir in the chilli powder and mixed spice and cook for 1 minute. Stir in the paprika and cook for 1 minute. Stir in the remaining ingredients, sausages and seasoning. Bring to the boil and cover and simmer for 30 minutes.

3. For the guacamole, scoop the avocado flesh into a bowl and mash with a fork. Stir in the spring onions, tomatoes, coriander and seasoning until well combined.

4. Serve the sausage casserole spooned into large hot bowls and top with soured cream and guacamole.

# Irish stew

1. Arrange the lamb, onions, carrots, swede, leeks and potatoes in layers, seasoning between each layer, in a large heavy-based pan. Pour over the stock and bring to the boil. Skim off any scum.

2. Bring back to the boil and cover and simmer for 2 hours, stirring occasionally. Stir in the thyme, cover and simmer for a further 1 hour, until the meat is tender. Serve garnished with more thyme and fresh crusty bread.

Preparation time: 20 min
Cooking time: 3 h
Serves 6

*1 kg stewing lamb or mutton, cut into pieces (middle or scrag end of neck)*
*2 large onions, thickly sliced*
*375g carrots, cut into large chunks*
*500g swede, cut into large chunks*
*2 leeks, sliced thickly*
*750g waxy potatoes, such as Desiree, cut into large chunks*
*1.75 litres hot lamb stock*
*a good bunch of thyme for garnish*

# Polenta with cheese and vegetable crust

**1.** Preheat the oven to 400°F (200°C). Butter a baking dish.

**2.** Heat the thyme and vegetable stock, and bring to a boil. Stir in the polenta and cook, stirring, for 10 minutes, until thick. Place in the baking dish, smoothing evenly.

**3.** Heat the oil in a frying pan and cook the shallot, garlic and pepper until softened. Stir in the paprika, cumin, cayenne, salt and pepper, and cook for 3 minutes.

**4.** Add the cheese, herbs and lemon zest.

**5.** Toss the courgettes in the lemon juice and a little salt, and place on the polenta.

**6.** Spoon the cheese mixture on top and bake for about 20 minutes until piping hot. Garnish with oregano.

Preparation time: 25 min
Cooking time: 20 min
Serves 4

*butter, for greasing*
*1 tsp dried thyme*
*500ml vegetable stock*
*180g polenta*
*2 tbsp olive oil*
*1 shallot, finely chopped*
*1 garlic clove, crushed*
*1 red pepper, diced*
*½ tsp paprika*
*1 pinch each of cumin and cayenne*
  *pepper*
*80g grated Gruyère cheese*
*2 tbsp chopped parsley*
*1 tbsp chopped oregano*
*1 lemon, juice and finely grated zest*
*200g courgettes, cut into thin strips*
*oregano sprigs to garnish*

# Rice casserole with pecorino

**1.** Preheat the oven to 350°F (180°C). Butter a baking dish.

**2.** Put the rice, salt and water in a pan and bring to the boil. Cover and cook for 15–18 minutes until the water is absorbed. Fluff with a fork and set aside.

**3.** Mix together the butter, cheese, onion, parsley, egg, milk and pepper. Stir into the rice and mix well.

**4.** Press into the baking dish and top with the tomatoes.

**5.** Bake for 35–40 minutes until the tomatoes are browned. Stand for 20 minutes before cutting.

**6.** Garnish with sage leaves.

Preparation time: 25 min
Cooking time: 1 h
Serves 4

*50g butter, melted, plus extra for greasing*
*200g long grain rice*
*1 tsp salt*
*500ml water*
*110g grated Pecorino cheese*
*2 tbsp chopped onion*
*4 tbsp chopped parsley*
*1 egg, beaten*
*125ml milk*
*¼ tsp pepper*
*4 tomatoes, sliced*
*sage leaves, to garnish*

# Asparagus and potato casserole with shrimps

Preparation time: 20 min
Cooking time: 50 min
Serves 4

*butter, for greasing*
*800g asparagus, cut into pieces*
*1kg new potatoes*
*160g shrimps*
*2 eggs*
*400ml low-fat milk*
*6 tbsp grated Gouda cheese*
*parsley sprigs, to serve*

**1.** Preheat the oven to 400°F (200°C). Butter a baking dish.

**2.** Cook the asparagus in boiling salted water for 10 minutes, then drain well.

**3.** Cook the potatoes in boiling salted water for 20 minutes and drain well. Cut into slices.

**4.** Layer the potato slices with the asparagus and shrimps in the baking dish.

**5.** Whisk the eggs with the milk and salt and pepper and pour over the layers in the dish. Sprinkle with cheese.

**6.** Bake for about 30 minutes until piping hot. Garnish with parsley.

# Beef goulash with homemade noodles

**1.** Preheat the oven to 300°F (150°C).

**2.** Heat the oil in a flameproof casserole dish and brown the meat in batches. Remove and set aside.

**3.** Add the onions and garlic to the dish, and cook for a few minutes until brown. Add the bouquet garni, salt, pepper and paprika with just enough stock to cover the meat.

**4.** Bring to the boil, cover and cook in the oven for about 2 hours until the meat is tender.

**5.** Scatter over the sage leaves and serve with noodles.

Preparation time: 20 min
Cooking time: 2 h 20 min
Serves 4

*2 tbsp oil*
*1kg stewing beef, cubed*
*2 large onions, sliced*
*1–2 garlic cloves, crushed*
*1 bouquet garni*
*1 tbsp paprika*
*stock, to cover the meat*
*sage leaves, to serve*
*cooked noodles, to serve*

# Miso stew with belly pork, beetroot and morels

**1.** Preheat the oven to 350°F (180°C).

**2.** Heat the oil in a flameproof casserole dish and fry the pork and bacon in batches till brown. Add the onion to the dish and cook for a few minutes until soft.

**3.** Stir in the stock and peppercorns. Add the beetroot and the morels and their soaking water.

**4.** Cover and cook in the oven for 1–1½ hours until the meat and beetroot are tender.

**5.** Spoon out a little of the liquid into a bowl and stir in the miso paste. Stir the sauce into the casserole and garnish with strips of red pepper.

Preparation time: 20 min
Cooking time: 1 h 45 min
Serves 4

*2 tbsp oil*
*800g belly pork, cubed*
*125g bacon diced*
*1 onion, finely chopped*
*300ml pork stock*
*6 black peppercorns*
*8 small beetroot, halved*
*100g dried morels, soaked in warm*
    *water for at least 30 minutes*
*2–3 tbsp miso paste*
*red pepper strips, to serve*

# White bean stew with lamb meatballs

**1.** Preheat the oven to 350°F (180°C).

**2.** Heat the oil in a flameproof casserole dish and fry the onion and garlic until translucent. Stir in the tomato purée and meat stock, and add the rosemary.

**3.** Add the beans and chickpeas, and season to taste with salt and pepper.

**4.** For the meatballs: mix the lamb with the egg, breadcrumbs (using more or less as necessary), parsley and sage. Season with salt and pepper. Divide the meat into walnut-sized balls.

**5.** Heat the oil in a frying pan and fry the meatballs until they are browned.

**6.** Add the meatballs to the casserole. Cover and cook in the oven for 30–40 minutes until piping hot.

Preparation time: 20 min
Cooking time: 45 min
Serves 4

*3 tbsp olive oil*
*1 large onion, chopped*
*5 garlic cloves, finely chopped*
*2 tbsp tomato purée*
*750ml meat stock*
*1 tsp chopped rosemary*
*400g white canned beans, e. g*
*    butter beans or cannellini beans*
*400g canned chickpeas, drained*

*For the meatballs:*
*500g minced (ground) lamb*
*1 egg*
*50g breadcrumbs*
*1 tbsp finely chopped parsley*
*5 sage leaves, finely chopped*
*2 tbsp oil*

# Rich seafood stew

**1.** Heat the oil in a flameproof casserole dish. Add the onions, pepper and squid, and cook on a low flame for 15 minutes, until softened.

**2.** Add the tomatoes, stock and tomato paste. Bring to a boil.

**3.** Stir in the prawns and place the pieces of fillet on top. Season to taste with salt and pepper. Push the pieces into the juices, then cover and cook in the oven for 20–30 minutes until the fish is cooked through.

**4.** Garnish with parsley.

Preparation time: 15 min
Cooking time: 45 min
Serves 4

*6 tbsp olive oil*
*2 onions, finely chopped*
*1 red pepper, chopped*
*450g squid*
*2 x 400g cans chopped tomatoes*
*500ml fish stock*
*2 tbsp sundried tomato paste*
*250g raw peeled prawns*
*1kg white fish fillets, cut into large*
  *pieces*
*a handful of parsley sprigs to*
  *garnish*

# Lamb stew with carrots, potatoes and mashed potatoes

**1.** Preheat the oven to 350°F (180°C).

**2.** Heat the oil in a flameproof casserole dish and brown the meat on all sides. Remove the meat and set aside.

**3.** Add the vegetables to the dish and cook for 5 minutes. Add the flour and cook for 1 minute, stirring.

**4.** Pour in the wine and season to taste with salt and pepper. Add the meat and bring to the boil.

**5.** Cover and cook in the oven for 1–2 hours until the lamb is tender. Serve with mashed potatoes.

Preparation time: 20 min
Cooking time: 2 h
Serves 4

*2 tbsp oil*
*800g boneless stewing lamb, cubed*
*1 onion, chopped*
*4 large potatoes, peeled and chopped*
*6 carrots, sliced*
*1 stick celery, chopped*
*2 tbsp flour*
*500ml red wine*
*mashed potatoes, to serve*

# Kale stew with potatoes, bacon and oat flakes

Preparation time: 20 min
Cooking time: 1 h 20 min
Serves 4

butter, for greasing
800g kale or green cabbage,
    chopped
400g potatoes, peeled and diced
1 large onion, chopped
3 bay leaves
2 tbsp oatmeal
50g butter
200g crisply cooked smoked
    streaky bacon, chopped
a handful of parsley sprigs to
    garnish

**1.** Preheat the oven to 375°F (190°C). Grease a baking dish.

**2.** Cook the cabbage, potatoes and onion in boiling salted water for 5 minutes.

**3.** Drain and season with salt and pepper. Put into the baking dish with the bay leaves and oatmeal.

**4.** Cover and cook for about 1 hour until the vegetables are tender.

**5.** Dot with butter and cook, uncovered, for about 15 minutes until lightly browned. Add the cooked bacon and garnish with parsley.

# Pork stew with mushrooms and peppers

**1.** Preheat the oven to 375°F (190°C).

**2.** Heat the oil in a flameproof casserole dish and brown the pork in batches. Remove from the dish and set aside.

**3.** Add the onion, pepper and mushrooms to the dish and cook for 3 minutes until softened. Remove from the dish and set aside.

**4.** Sprinkle in the flour and cook, stirring, for 2 minutes. Stir in the wine and stock.

**5.** Add all the remaining ingredients to the dish and stir well.

**6.** Cover and cook for about 1–1 ½ hours until the pork is tender.

Preparation time: 20 min
Cooking time: 1 h 45 min
Serves 4

*2 tbsp oil*
*700g lean pork, cubed*
*1 onion, chopped*
*1 red pepper, chopped*
*225g mushrooms, sliced*
*2 tbsp flour*
*300ml white wine*
*150ml pork stock*
*2 tbsp tomato purée*
*500g canned tomatoes*
*2 tsp chopped sage*

# Stracotto di capretto

**1.** Preheat the oven to 300°F (150°C).

**2.** Heat the oil in a flameproof casserole dish and brown the meat on all sides. Add the onion to the dish and cook until soft.

**3.** Sprinkle in the flour and cook for 1 minute. Stir in the stock, season to taste and bring to a boil.

**4.** Add 3 oregano sprigs, cover, and cook in the oven for 3–4 hours until the meat is very tender. Add the chestnuts for the last 25 minutes of the cooking time.

**5.** Garnish with the remaining oregano sprigs.

Preparation time: 15 min
Cooking time: 4 h 15 min
Serves 4

*60ml olive oil*
*1.5kg kid or lamb meat, cubed*
*1 onion, finely chopped*
*2 tbsp flour*
*400ml stock*
*6 oregano sprigs*
*240g pack chopped cooked*
  *chestnuts*

# Pork stew with onions

**1.** Preheat the oven to 350°F (180°C).

**2.** Heat the oil in a flameproof casserole dish and add the onion and pork. Cook for about 5 minutes until golden.

**3.** Stir in the paprika, followed by the tomatoes and stock. Season to taste with salt and pepper. Add the yellow peppers and the bay leaf.

**4.** Cover and cook in the oven for about 1–1 ½ hours, until the pork is tender.

Preparation time: 15 min
Cooking time: 1 h 40 min
Serves 4

*1 tbsp oil*
*3 large onions, roughly chopped*
*1kg lean pork belly, cut into 2.5cm*
*   pieces*
*1 tsp paprika*
*400g canned chopped tomatoes*
*450ml chicken or vegetable stock*
*2 yellow peppers, cut into wedges*
*1 bay leaf*

# Duck curry with dates

Preparation time: 20 min
Cooking time: 1 h 50 min
Serves 4–6

*6 duck legs*
*2 tbsp light brown sugar*
*4 tbsp red Thai curry paste*
*1 x 400ml canned coconut milk*
*1 can duck stock*
*2 tbsp fish sauce*
*150g dates, pitted*

**1.** Preheat the oven to 350°F (180°C).

**2.** Dry-fry the duck legs in a flameproof casserole dish for 10–15 minutes until browned. Remove from the dish and set aside.

**3.** Add the sugar to the fat in the dish and cook until caramelised. Add the curry paste and cook for few minutes until fragrant. Stir in the coconut milk and stock. Bring to the boil, stirring.

**4.** Stir in the fish sauce. Add the duck legs, cover and cook in the oven for 1 ½ hours, until the duck is tender. Add the dates for the last 30 minutes of cooking.

# Vegetable stew with shiitake and sesame balls

**1.** Put the vegetables into a flameproof casserole dish with the soy sauce, salt and stock. Bring to the boil and cook for 10 minutes until the vegetables are tender.

**2.** For the sesame balls, soak the bread in a little milk until absorbed.

**3.** Heat the butter in a pan and fry the onion until soft. Set aside to cool.

**4.** Squeeze the bread to remove the excess moisture and mix the bread with the onion, fish, salt and pepper. Stir in the eggs and coriander, mixing well. Add a little flour to make a firm mixture.

**5.** Beat the egg whites until frothy and stir in the cornflour.

**6.** Roll the fish balls in the egg white mixture, then in the sesame seeds. Cover the balls and chill.

**7.** Heat enough oil in a frying pan to cover the base and fry the sesame balls for about 3 minutes. Drain on kitchen paper.

**8.** Put the fish balls into the hot vegetables and serve immediately.

Preparation time: 20 min
Cooking time: 20 min
Serves 4

*100g carrots, thinly sliced*
*8 dried shiitake mushrooms, soaked*
  *in warm water for 30 minutes*
*100g sugar snap peas*
*1 leek, sliced*
*1 red chilli, finely chopped*
*80ml soy sauce*
*1 pinch salt*
*700ml vegetable stock*

*For the sesame balls:*
*2 slices bread*
*milk*
*1 tbsp butter*
*1 onion, finely chopped*
*600g cod fillet, minced*
*2 eggs*
*3 tbsp chopped coriander*
*flour*
*2 egg whites*
*2 tbsp cornflour*
*100g sesame seeds*
*oil*

# Gumbo stew

**1.** Preheat the oven to 350°F (180°C).

**2.** Mix together the spices, salt and peppers.

**3.** Sprinkle the chicken with 1 tablespoon of the mix and sprinkle the prawns with another 1 tablespoon of the mix.

**4.** Heat the oil in a flameproof casserole dish and cook the onion until softened. Add the seasoned chicken and cook for 2 minutes. Add the bay leaves and tomatoes, and the remaining spice mixture. Cook until most of the liquid is absorbed.

**5.** Add the flour and stir until it is completely absorbed. Cook for 1 minute.

**6.** Add the stock, stir well and bring to a boil.

**7.** Add the seasoned prawns and rice. Cover and cook in the oven for about 15–20 minutes until the prawns are pink and plump. Sprinkle over the parsley and black pepper before serving.

Preparation time: 20 min
Cooking time: 40 min
Serves 4

*2 tsp paprika*
*2 tsp English mustard powder*
*1 tsp dried basil*
*½ tsp salt*
*1 tsp onion salt*
*1 tsp garlic salt*
*1 tsp dried thyme*
*1 tsp dried oregano*
*1 tsp black pepper*
*1 pinch cayenne pepper*
*400g boneless chicken breasts,*
*    thickly sliced*
*400g prawns, peeled and deveined*
*2 tbsp oil*
*1 onion, chopped*
*2 bay leaves*
*400ml canned chopped tomatoes*
*2 tbsp flour*
*600ml fish stock*
*450g cooked rice*
*a handful of chopped parsley to*
*    garnish.*

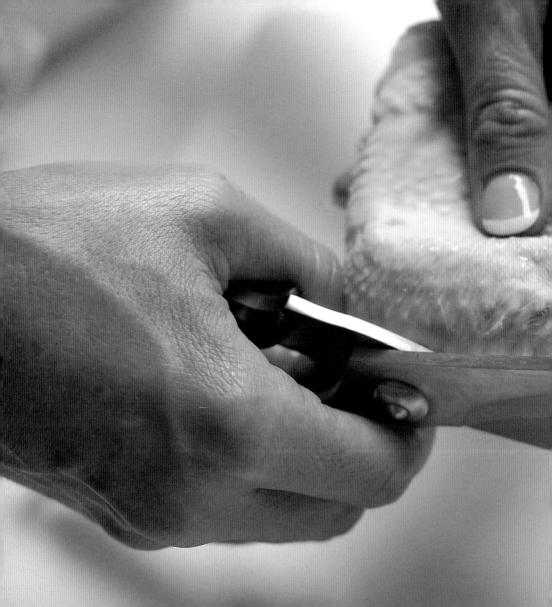

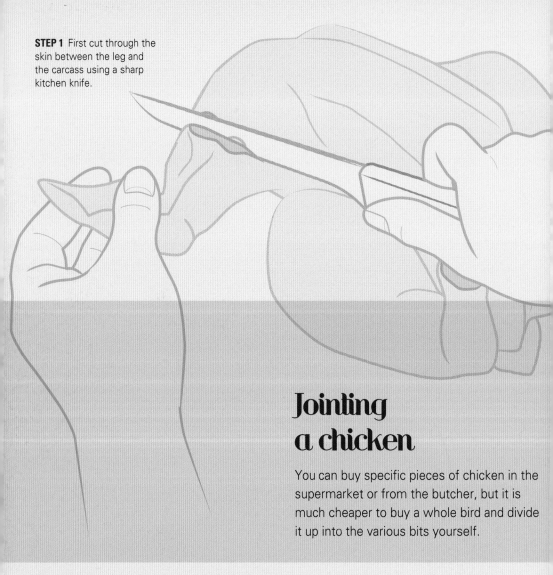

**STEP 1** First cut through the skin between the leg and the carcass using a sharp kitchen knife.

# Jointing a chicken

You can buy specific pieces of chicken in the supermarket or from the butcher, but it is much cheaper to buy a whole bird and divide it up into the various bits yourself.

**STEP 2** Bend the leg away from the carcass as far as you can – the joint should pop out. Cut it away from the backbone and repeat with the other leg.

**STEP 3** Divide each leg piece into two by cutting through the joint just above the drumstick. Press the knife down hard to slice through cleanly.

**STEP 4** Using a sharp knife or scissors, cut away the breast from the ribs and the backbone to create a fillet.

**STEP 5** Once jointed, you should be left with leg and thigh pieces as well as drumsticks and breast fillets.

# Shrimp gratin

**1.** Preheat the oven to 375°F (190°C). Grease a baking dish.

**2.** Heat the oil in a pan and fry the onion and garlic until soft. Stir in the spices, tomatoes and sugar, and simmer for 15 minutes.

**3.** Stir in the shrimps, salt and pepper, and transfer to the baking dish.

**4.** Sprinkle with the cheese and oregano and bake for 15–20 minutes until piping hot.

Preparation time: 20 min
Cooking time: 40 min
Serves 4

*2 tbsp olive oil*
*1 onion, chopped*
*2 garlic cloves, finely chopped*
*½ tsp ground cinnamon*
*¼ tsp allspice*
*2 x 400g cans chopped tomatoes*
*¼ tsp sugar*
*600g shrimps, peeled and deveined*
*¼ tsp salt*
*¼ tsp pepper*
*110g crumbled Feta cheese*
*1 tbsp chopped oregano*

# Cassoulet de Toulouse

**1.** Preheat the oven to 300°F (150°C).

**2.** Drain the beans and place them in a pan of fresh cold water. Bring the beans to a boil and cook for 5 minutes.

**3.** Drain the beans and tip them into a pan. Add the diced pork rind and bacon and cover with fresh cold water. Bring to the boil and cook for 10 minutes. Drain the beans, rind and bacon.

**4.** Heat the duck fat in a large flameproof casserole dish and cook the celery, onion, carrot and garlic for 5 minutes.

**5.** Add the thyme, cloves and bay leaves, and continue cooking slowly for another 5 minutes. Add the sausage and cook until browned.

**6.** Remove as much fat as possible from the confit duck and add the duck pieces to the pan with the beans, pork rind and bacon. Pour in enough water to cover all the ingredients, then bring to a boil and skim off the scum. Season to taste with salt and pepper.

**7.** Cook uncovered in the oven for 2–4 hours, stirring occasionally until the beans are soft and creamy and the cassoulet has thickened. If the cassoulet looks as if it's drying out while cooking, add more water.

Preparation time: 20 min
Cooking time: 4 h 20 min
Serves 4

*700g haricot beans, soaked*
   *overnight in water*
*75g pork rind, diced*
*125g smoked streaky bacon, diced*
*2 tbsp duck fat (from the confit)*
*1 stick celery, roughly chopped*
*1 onion, roughly chopped*
*1 carrot, roughly chopped*
*2 garlic cloves, crushed*
*3 sprigs thyme*
*3 cloves*
*3 bay leaves*
*350g garlic sausage, thickly sliced*
*350g duck confit*

# Braised veal shank with spinach and chickpeas

**1.** Preheat the oven to 280°F (140°C).

**2.** Mix salt and pepper in the flour and toss the veal shanks until they are evenly coated.

**3.** Heat the oil in a frying pan and brown the veal shanks on all sides. Set aside.

**4.** Add the onion and garlic to the pan and cook until soft, but not browned. Stir in the tomato purée and bay leaf.

**5.** Put the contents of the pan and the veal shanks into a large casserole dish.

**6.** Add the wine to the pan and bring to a boil. Stir in the stock and pour into the casserole dish. Cover and cook for about 3 hours, until the veal is tender.

**7.** Heat the butter in a pan and quickly cook the spinach until it begins to wilt. Season to taste with salt, pepper and nutmeg, and drain well. Stir in the chickpeas. Add the ingredients to the casserole dish for the last 10 minutes of cooking time.

Preparation time: 20 min
Cooking time: 3 h 25 min
Serves 4

*4 veal shanks*
*3 tbsp flour*
*2 tbsp olive oil*
*1 onion, finely chopped*
*2 garlic cloves, finely chopped*
*4 tsp tomato purée*
*1 bay leaf*
*100ml dry white wine*
*500ml veal or beef stock*
*50g butter*
*400g spinach*
*1 pinch grated nutmeg*
*1 x 400g can chickpeas, drained*

# Salmon gratin with herbs and potatoes

Preparation time: 25 min
Cooking time: 45 min
Serves 4

*500g potatoes, peeled and thinly sliced*
*250g smoked salmon, thinly sliced*
*4 eggs*
*200ml double cream*
*3 tbsp mixed, chopped herbs*
*50g grated Parmesan cheese*
*grated nutmeg*

**1.** Heat the oven to 400°F (200°C). Butter a baking dish.

**2.** Put one-third of the potatoes in the baking dish and sprinkle with salt and pepper.

**3.** Place half the salmon on top and cover with another third of the potato slices. Season with salt and pepper. Add the remaining salmon and cover with potatoes. Season with salt and pepper.

**4.** Beat the eggs with the cream, stir in the herbs and cheese and season with salt, pepper and nutmeg. Pour over the layers in the baking dish and bake for 45 minutes until browned and bubbling.

# Braised beef with onions and carrots

1. Preheat the oven to 300°F (150°C).

2. Season the beef with salt and pepper.

3. Heat 2 tablespoon oil in a flameproof casserole dish and brown the meat on all sides. Remove from the dish and set aside.

4. Briefly cook the shallots, garlic and the rest of the vegetables in the remaining oil. Stir in the tomato puree and deglaze with red wine. Boil until reduced.

5. Repeat the process with the port. Add a little stock, the balsamic vinegar and bay leaf and return the meat to the dish.

6. Cook for 2–2 ½ hours, turning the meat frequently and gradually adding the rest of the stock. Finally, season to taste with salt and pepper.

Preparation time: 20 min
Cooking time: 2 h 45 min
Serves 6–8

1.5kg beef (e.g shoulder)
3 tbsp oil
8 shallots
2 garlic cloves
2 carrots, roughly chopped
1 parsley root, roughly chopped
200g celeriac, roughly chopped
1 tbsp tomato purée
200ml red wine
100ml port wine
750ml beef stock
2 tbsp balsamic vinegar
1 bay leaf

# Braised lamb

**1.** Preheat the oven to 350°F (180°C).

**2.** Mix salt and pepper in the flour. Toss the lamb to coat the pieces evenly with the seasoned flour.

**3.** Heat the oil in a frying pan and fry the onions till brown. Add the meat, a few pieces at a time.

**4.** Transfer the onions and meat to a casserole dish, together with the carrots.

**5.** Pour the stock into the frying pan, bring to the boil, scraping up any residue stuck to the pan. Boil until the stock reduces slightly and pour it over the meat and vegetables.

**6.** Cover and cook in the oven for about 1 ½ hours, until the meat is tender. Add the tomatoes, sweetcorn and mint for the last 15 minutes of cooking time.

Preparation time: 20 min
Cooking time: 1 h 45 min
Serves 4

*1 tbsp flour*
*½ tsp pepper*
*½ tsp salt*
*1kg boneless lamb, cubed*
*1 tbsp oil*
*1 onion, sliced*
*4 carrots, chopped*
*200–300ml lamb stock*
*4 large tomatoes, quartered*
*4 tbsp canned sweetcorn, drained*
*2 tbsp chopped mint*

# Beef cheek casserole

**1.** Preheat the oven to 300°F (150°C).

**2.** Mix the salt and pepper in the flour. Add the meat and coat it evenly.

**3.** Heat the oil in a flameproof casserole dish and brown the meat on all sides. Remove the meat from the dish and set aside.

**4.** Add the onions, carrots, peppers and bacon to the dish and cook until it starts turning brown. Remove from the heat. Add the bay leaf and chopped thyme with the meat.

**5.** Pour in the stock and wine and cook for 2½–3 hours until the meat is tender. Garnish with the thyme sprig.

Preparation time: 20 min
Cooking time: 3 h 20 min
Serves 4

*2 tbsp plain flour*
*1kg ox cheeks*
*2 tbsp olive oil*
*2 onions, chopped*
*500g carrots, chopped*
*2 red peppers, chopped*
*2 smoked bacon rashers, diced*
*1 bay leaf*
*1 tbsp chopped thyme*
*300ml beef stock*
*400ml red wine*
*1 sprig of thyme, to garnish*

# Veal goulash

Preparation time: 20 min
Cooking time: 1 h 30 min
Serves 4

*1 tbsp oil*
*1kg boneless veal shoulder, cubed*
*1 onion, chopped*
*2 red peppers, cut into strips*
*2 garlic cloves, crushed*
*3 tbsp paprika*
*¼ tsp caraway seeds*
*400g canned chopped tomatoes*
*400ml veal or beef stock*
*wide ribbon noodles, to serve*
*fresh thyme, to garnish*

**1.** Preheat the oven to 350°F (180°C).

**2.** Heat the oil in a flameproof casserole dish and brown the meat in batches. Remove from the dish and set aside.

**3.** Add the onion, peppers and garlic to the dish, and cook until just softened. Stir in the paprika and caraway seeds.

**4.** Add the meat and tomatoes to the dish and season to taste with salt and pepper. Pour in the stock and bring to a boil.

**5.** Cover and cook in the oven for 1–1¼ hours, until the meat is tender. Garnish with thyme and serve the veal with wide ribbon noodles.

# Braised chicken with parsnips and herbs

Preparation time: 20 min
Cooking time: 1 h 45 min
Serves 4

*4 chicken thighs*
*4 chicken drumsticks*
*2 tbsp olive oil*
*4 shallots, chopped*
*2 garlic cloves, crushed*
*1 small leek, sliced*
*2 carrots, chopped*
*600g parsnips, chopped*
*100ml dry white wine*
*600–800ml hot chicken stock*
*2 bay leaves*
*5 juniper berries*
*4 sage leaves*
*10 sprigs thyme*
*150ml double cream*

**1.** Preheat the oven to 350°F (180°C).

**2.** Rub the chicken pieces with salt and pepper.

**3.** Heat the oil in a flameproof casserole dish and brown the chicken. Remove and set aside.

**4.** Add the vegetables and cook for a few minutes until soft.

**5.** Deglaze the vegetables with the wine and pour in the hot chicken stock. Add the bay leaf and juniper berries, and bring to a boil.

**6.** Add the chicken, sage and 4 sprigs of thyme.

**7.** Cover and cook in the oven for 1–1 ½ hours until the chicken is tender.

**8.** Remove the bay leaves and stir in the cream. Season to taste with salt and pepper. Garnish with the remaining thyme.

# Asian chicken and noodle stew

**1.** Preheat the oven to 350°F (180°C).

**2.** Put the chicken in a flameproof casserole dish and pour in the chicken stock to cover the meat. Bring to a boil and cook for 2 minutes.

**3.** Add the vegetables, mushrooms and their soaking water, salt and pepper. Bring to a boil.

**4.** Mix the cornflour with a little water to a paste and stir into the casserole with the peas and noodles.

**5.** Cover and cook for 20–30 minutes until the chicken is cooked.

Preparation time: 20 min
Cooking time: 45 min
Serves 4

4 chicken breasts, thickly sliced
chicken stock
2 sticks celery, chopped
1 onion, chopped
4 carrots, diced
40g dried Chinese mushrooms,
    soaked in warm water for
    20 minutes
1 tbsp salt
2 tsp pepper
2 tbsp cornflour
200g peas
225g cooked egg noodles

# Browning meat

Cooking meat before adding it to a casserole not only gives it a deeper colour but also a stronger flavour. It is a simple technique that makes all the difference.

**STEP 1** First remove the membrane and any excess fat or gristle from your piece of meat.

**STEP 2** Slice the pieces of meat into long, thick, even slices using a sharp kitchen knife.

**STEP 3** When all the meat is cut into strips, slice across them to create even-sized cubes.

**STEP 4** Heat the oil and butter in a frying pan until hot then add the meat – you may need to do this in batches.

**STEP 5** When the meat is browned on all sides, add a sprinkling of flour to the pan to soak up all the meat juices.

# Beef casserole with dumplings

**1.** Put the meat, onions and carrots into a large bowl. Combine the spices with the cider vinegar and sugar and pour over the beef. Cover and leave to stand overnight, turning the meat from time to time.

**2.** Preheat the oven to 300°F (150°C). Transfer the contents of the bowl to a flameproof casserole dish and pour in the stock. Stir in the bay leaves and salt. Bring to a boil.

**3.** Cover and cook in the oven for 2–2 ½ hours until the meat is tender.

**4.** For the dumplings, mix the flour and suet in a mixing bowl. Season with salt and pepper. Stir in just enough water to form a soft dough. Roll into small balls with floured hands and place in the casserole for the last 25 minutes of cooking time.

Preparation time: 25 min
  plus overnight marinating
Cooking time: 2 h 30 min
Serves 4

*900g stewing steak, cubed*
*2 onions, sliced*
*4 carrots, roughly chopped*
*1 pinch ground cloves*
*1 pinch ground mace*
*5 black peppercorns*
*75ml cider vinegar*
*1 tbsp dark brown sugar*
*600ml beef stock*
*2 bay leaves*
*½ tsp salt*

*For the dumplings:*
*110g self-raising flour*
*50g shredded suet*

# Meat and cabbage stew with potato crust

**1.** Preheat the oven to 300°F (150°C).

**2.** Heat 2 tablespoons oil in a flameproof casserole dish and brown the meat in batches. Remove from the dish and set aside.

**3.** Add the garlic and onions to the dish and cook for 2 minutes until just softened.

**4.** Add the cabbage, sage, salt and pepper and the meat. Pour in the wine and just enough stock to cover the contents of the dish.

**5.** Cover and cook in the oven for 2 hours. Remove from the oven and increase the oven temperature to 400°F (200°C).

**6.** Put the potato slices in a bowl with 1 teaspoon of salt and the remaining oil. Fry well and place it on top of the casserole.

**7.** Cook for about 30 minutes, until the potatoes are tender. Sprinkle the cheese on top and cook for a further 15–20 minutes until the cheese has melted.

Preparation time: 25 min
Cooking time: 3 h
Serves 4

4 tbsp oil
1kg stewing beef, cubed
1 garlic clove, crushed
2 onions, sliced
450g cabbage, shredded
6 sage leaves, crushed lightly
1 tsp salt
220ml white wine
beef stock
900g potatoes, peeled and thinly
   sliced
225g grated Fontina cheese

# Beef, sausage and vegetable stew

**1.** Preheat the oven to 300°F (150°C).

**2.** Heat the oil in a flameproof casserole dish and brown the meat in batches. Remove and set aside.

**3.** Add the onions, leeks and celery to the dish and cook for 5 minutes.

**4.** Add the remaining ingredients with the meat and stir well.

**5.** Cover and cook for 2–2 ½ hours until the meat is tender.

Preparation time: 20 min
Cooking time: 3 h
Serves 4

*2 tbsp oil*
*500g stewing beef, cubed*
*2 onions, chopped*
*2 leeks, sliced*
*1 stick celery, chopped*
*500g garlic sausage, thickly sliced*
*2 pickled cucumbers, cut into strips*
*100ml water*
*1 tsp salt*
*1 litre beef stock*
*200g canned chopped tomatoes*
*2 tbsp tomato purée*
*1 bay leaf*
*black peppercorns*

# Mackerel and potato bake

Preparation time: 25 min
Cooking time: 45 min
Serves 4

*1kg waxy potatoes, peeled and
    thinly sliced*
*500ml milk*
*75ml crème fraîche*
*2 tbsp oil*
*1 onion, chopped*
*1 garlic clove, crushed*
*100ml dry white wine*

**1.** Heat the oven to 350°F (180°C). Grease a baking dish.

**2.** Arrange the potatoes in the baking dish in neat layers,
seasoning each layer with salt and pepper.

**3.** Whisk together the milk and crème fraîche, season with salt
and pepper and pour over the potatoes.

**4.** Cook for about 25 minutes, until golden brown.

**5.** Heat the oil in a pan and fry the onion until translucent.
Add the garlic and stir in the white wine. Cook until the wine
is reduced by half.

**6.** Place the fish on top of the potatoes in the baking dish.
Pour the onion and white wine mixture over it and season
with salt and pepper. Bake for a further 15–20 minutes until
the mackerel are cooked.

# Date and sausage stew

**1.** Preheat the oven to 350°F (180°C).

**2.** Heat 1 tablespoon oil in a flameproof casserole dish and brown the sausage slices. Add the onion, garlic and red pepper and cook until just softened. Remove and set aside.

**3.** Heat the remaining oil in the dish and brown the potato slices, sweet potatoes and courgettes. Add the sausages, onion, garlic and pepper to the dish and season with salt and pepper.

**4.** Pour in the wine and passata, and stir in the sugar and paprika. Cover and cook for about 30 minutes until the vegetables are tender.

**5.** Add the chickpeas and dates and cook for a further 10–15 minutes until piping hot.

Preparation time: 20 min
Cooking time: 1 h
Serves 4

*3 tbsp olive oil*
*8 pork sausages, thickly sliced*
*1 onion, chopped*
*2 garlic cloves, chopped*
*1 red pepper, chopped*
*4 potatoes, thinly sliced*
*2 sweet potatoes, cut into small*
    *chunks*
*4 courgettes, thickly sliced*
*150ml red wine*
*680ml passata*
*1 tsp sugar*
*½ tsp paprika*
*400g canned chickpeas, drained*
*8 dates, split in half*

# Boeuf bourguignon

**1.** Preheat the oven to 300°F (150°C).

**2.** Heat the oil in a large frying pan and brown the meat cubes in batches. Put into a casserole dish.

**3.** Add the bacon, onions, parsnips, carrots, celery and garlic to the pan and cook briefly until just browned. Put into the casserole dish.

**4.** Pour in the brandy and red wine. Season to taste with salt and pepper and stir everything together. Cover tightly and cook for about 3 hours until the meat is very tender.

**5.** Sprinkle with chopped parsley.

Preparation time: 15 min
Cooking time: 3 h 20 min
Serves 4

*2 tbsp oil*
*750g stewing steak, cubed*
*100g diced streaky bacon*
*300g small onions*
*4 parsnips, roughly chopped*
*4 carrots, chopped*
*1 stick celery, chopped*
*2 garlic cloves, crushed*
*55ml brandy or Cognac*
*500ml robust red wine*
*2 tbsp chopped parsley, to serve*

# Hungarian goulash

**1.** Preheat the oven to 300°F (150°C).

**2.** Heat the oil in a flameproof casserole dish and cook the onions, peppers, garlic and salt for 5 minutes until soft. Remove and set aside.

**3.** Add the beef to the dish and brown on all sides.

**4.** Add the onions, peppers and garlic to the dish with the caraway seeds and paprika. Add just enough stock to cover the contents of the dish. Cover and cook for 1 hour.

**5.** Add the potatoes and cook for a further hour.

**6.** Add the tomatoes to the dish and cook for a further 20–30 minutes. Sprinkle with parsley and garnish with parsley sprigs.

Preparation time: 20 min
Cooking time: 2 h 40 min
Serves 4

*60ml oil*
*200g onions, finely chopped*
*2 red peppers, chopped*
*1 garlic clove, finely chopped*
*1 ½ tsp salt*
*750g lean stewing steak, cubed*
*1 pinch caraway seeds*
*1 ½ tbsp Hungarian paprika*
*beef stock*
*1kg potatoes, peeled and diced*
*150g tomatoes, quartered*
*2–3 tbsp chopped parsley,*
*a few parsley sprigs, to garnish*

# Sea bream braised in olive oil with olives and tomatoes

Preparation time: 5 min
Cooking time: 35 min
Serves 4

*4 gilthead bream*
*1 lemon zest, grated*
*200ml olive oil*
*200g cherry tomatoes*
*100g black olives, pitted*
*2 sprigs basil, to garnish*

**1.** Preheat the oven to 400°F (200°C).

**2.** Place the bream in a baking dish and sprinkle with salt, pepper and lemon zest.

**3.** Pour in the oil and add the tomatoes and olives. Cover and cook for 20–30 minutes, until the fish is cooked. Garnish with basil.

# Cataplana (Portuguese fish stew)

**1.** Preheat the oven to 375°F (190°C).

**2.** Put the tomatoes into a pan of boiling water for a few seconds and refresh in cold water. Skin the tomatoes and then roughly dice them.

**3.** Heat 2 tablespoons oil in a flameproof casserole dish and fry the onions and garlic until translucent. Add the tomatoes and peppers, and cook briefly.

**4.** Stir in the white wine, add the bay leaves and chilli, and simmer for 10 minutes.

**5.** Place the fish and shellfish on top of the vegetables. Season with salt and pepper and drizzle with the remaining oil.

**6.** Cover and cook in the oven for 20–30 minutes, until the fish is cooked.

Preparation time: 15 min
Cooking time: 50 min
Serves 8

*6 tomatoes*
*50ml olive oil*
*2 onions, chopped*
*4 garlic cloves, crushed*
*2 green peppers, chopped*
*200ml white wine*
*2 bay leaves*
*1 chilli, finely chopped*
*2kg fish of your choice, cut
  into chunks*
*1kg shellfish of your choice,
  e. g. clams*

# Potato and ham gratin

**1.** Preheat the oven to 350°F (180°C). Butter a 2-litre gratin dish.

**2.** Heat the stock, cream and milk in a pan with the garlic and bay leaf and bring to the boil. Remove from the heat, cover and leave to stand.

**3.** Mix the potatoes, leeks and ham together in the dish, and spread out in an even layer. Pour over the stock mixture. Season with salt and pepper and sprinkle with the cheese.

**4.** Loosely cover with foil and bake for 30 minutes. Remove the foil and bake for a further 30–40 minutes, spooning some of the stock mixture over occasionally, until the potatoes are tender. Allow to stand for 10 minutes before serving.

Preparation time: 20 min
Cooking time: 1 h 15 min
Serves 4

*1 tbsp butter*
*125ml vegetable stock*
*300ml double cream*
*150ml milk*
*1 garlic clove, crushed*
*1 bay leaf*
*800g potatoes, peeled and thinly sliced*
*2 leeks, thinly sliced*
*175g cooked ham, chopped*
*85g grated cheese*

# Braised pork with vegetables

**1.** Heat the oven to 400°F (200°C).

**2.** Put all the vegetables, except the sweetcorn into a casserole dish. Mix the tomato paste and stock and pour into the dish.

**3.** Cover and cook for 30 minutes. Remove from the oven and increase the oven temperature to 425°F (220°C).

**4.** Place the pork chops on top of the vegetables and cook for about 25 minutes, until the chops are cooked and brown. Add the sweetcorn for the last 5 minutes of cooking time.

Preparation time: 15 min
Cooking time: 1 h 15 min
Serves 4

*12 new potatoes*
*4 sticks celery, cut into 5-cm lengths*
*8 spring carrots*
*4 garlic cloves*
*2 onions, quartered*
*225g French beans, sliced*
*1 tbsp sundried tomato paste*
*300ml hot pork stock*
*4 bone-in pork loin chops*
*6 tbsp canned sweetcorn, drained*

# Pot au feu

**1.** Preheat the oven to 325°F (160°C).

**2.** Season the chicken pieces well.

**3.** Heat the oil in a large frying pan and brown the chicken pieces on all sides.

**4.** Add the thyme, bay leaves and garlic, stir briefly with the chicken, then add the stock.

**5.** Bring to a boil, add the vegetables and transfer to a casserole dish. Season to taste with salt and pepper.

**6.** Cook for about 1 hour until the chicken is cooked and the vegetables are tender.

Preparation time: 15 min
Cooking time: 1 h
Serves 4

*1 chicken, cut into 8 pieces*
*4 tbsp olive oil*
*1 tbsp thyme*
*2 bay leaves*
*1 garlic clove, finely diced*
*200ml chicken stock*
*8 spring onions, chopped*
*250g green asparagus, trimmed and*
   *cut into smaller pieces*
*200g small carrots, washed*
*400g small potatoes, scrubbed*

# Fricassee of poularde breast with peas and morels

**1.** Preheat the oven to 350°F (180°C).

**2.** Heat the oil and butter in a flameproof casserole dish and quickly brown the chicken. Add the shallot and drained morels and cook for 2 minutes.

**3.** Stir in the flour and cook for 1 minute. Add the stock and cream and the morel soaking water. Stir in the peas and lemon juice and season to taste with salt and pepper.

**4.** Cover and cook in the oven for 30–40 minutes until the chicken is cooked and tender.

Preparation time: 15 min
Cooking time: 55 min
Serves 4

*1 tbsp sunflower oil*
*1 tbsp butter*
*4 chicken breasts, thickly sliced*
*1 shallot, chopped*
*30g dried morels, soaked in warm*
*    water for 30 minutes*
*1 tbsp flour*
*400ml chicken stock*
*150ml double cream*
*150g peas*
*1 tbsp lemon juice*

# Daube de boeuf

Preparation time: 20 min
Cooking time: 2 h 50 min
Serves 4

*2 tbsp oil*
*1kg stewing beef, cut into 5-cm*
*    cubes*
*750g carrots, thickly sliced*
*4 onions, quartered*
*3 garlic cloves, finely chopped*
*1 litre red wine*
*100ml brandy*
*1 bouquet garni*
*rosemary sprigs, to serve*

**1.** Preheat the oven to 300°F (150°C).

**2.** Heat the oil in a large flameproof casserole dish and quickly brown the meat in batches. Set the meat aside.

**3.** In the same casserole dish, add the carrots, onions and garlic and cook for a few minutes until browned. Return the meat to the pan and add the red wine and brandy stirring well.

**4.** Season with salt and pepper, add the bouquet garni, cover and bring to a boil.

**5.** Cover and cook in the oven for about 2½ hours until the meat is tender. Garnish with rosemary.

# Tuna bake

1. Heat the oven to 350°F (180°C). Grease a baking dish.

2. Boil the pasta for 2 minutes less time than stated on the pack.

3. Melt the butter in a pan and stir in the flour. Cook for 1 minute, then gradually stir in the milk to make a thick sauce. Remove from the heat and stir in most of the cheese.

4. Drain the pasta, mix with the sauce, tuna and sweetcorn. Season to taste with salt and pepper.

5. Transfer to the baking dish and sprinkle with the remaining grated cheese. Bake for 15–20 minutes until golden. Garnish with sage leaves.

Preparation time: 10 min
Cooking time: 30 min
Serves 4

*600g macaroni*
*50g butter*
*50g plain flour*
*600ml milk*
*200g grated sharp cheese*
*2 x 160g cans tuna steak, drained*
*330g canned sweetcorn, drained*
*sage leaves, to serve*

# Ossobuco

**1.** Preheat the oven to 350°F (180°C).

**2.** Heat the oil in a flameproof casserole dish. Dust the veal shins with flour on both sides and brown in the hot oil. Remove from the pan and set aside.

**3.** Add the butter to the dish and add the chopped vegetables with the salt to cook gently for a few minutes. When the vegetables are soft, return the meat to the dish and add the wine. Cook gently until the moisture is almost completely dried out.

**4.** Add the hot stock, cover and cook in the oven for 2–2 ½ hours until the meat is very tender. Sprinkle with the parsley.

**Tips:** When serving the ossi buchi make sure that you lift them gently, so that they stay in one piece and the marrow is not lost.

Preparation time: 20 min
Cooking time: 2 h 45 min
Serves 4

*2 tbsp olive oil*
*4 veal shins*
*flour, for dusting*
*1 tbsp butter*
*1 onion, chopped*
*3 carrots, chopped*
*1 stick celery, chopped*
*1 pinch salt*
*150ml dry white wine*
*300ml hot veal stock*
*2 tbsp chopped parsley*

# Beef ragout with chanterelle mushrooms

**1.** Preheat the oven to 300°F (150°C).

**2.** Coat the beef evenly with the flour.

**3.** Heat the oil in a flameproof casserole dish and brown the meat in batches. Remove the meat and set aside.

**4.** Add the onions and garlic to the dish and fry until brown. Pour in the port and some of the stock. Add the meat and season with salt and pepper and add the bay leaf. Cover and cook in the oven for 1 ½ hours.

**5.** Heat the butter in a pan and cook the mushrooms until just browned. Add the mushrooms to the casserole and cook for a further 30 minutes.

**6.** Sprinkle the chopped parsley over the top and serve.

Preparation time: 20 min
Cooking time: 2 h 15 min
Serves 4

1kg stewing beef, cubed
2 tbsp flour
2 tbsp oil
3 onions, chopped
2 garlic cloves, crushed
150ml port wine
250ml beef stock
1 bay leaf
2 tbsp butter
400g chanterelle mushrooms
2 tbsp chopped parsley, to garnish

# Chorizo stew

Preparation time: 20 min
Cooking time: 1 h
Serves 4

3 tbsp oil
2 onions, roughly chopped
2 garlic cloves
2 tsp paprika
250g chorizo, chopped
2 potatoes, peeled and diced
1 small carrot, peeled and
  chopped
3 tbsp tomato purée
900ml vegetable stock
1 bay leaf
1–2 tsp dried oregano
4 tbsp crème fraîche, to serve
parsley leaves, to garnish

**1.** Heat the oven to 375°F (190°C).

**2.** Heat the oil in a large pan and gently cook the onions until soft but not brown.

**3.** Add the garlic and paprika, cook for 2 minutes then add the chorizo and cook until the fat starts to run.

**4.** Add the potatoes and carrot, stir in the tomato purée then add then stock, bay leaf and oregano.

**5.** Bring to a boil, season with salt and pepper then transfer to a casserole dish.

**6.** Cover and cook for 45–60 minutes until the vegetables are tender.

**7.** Spoon over the creme fraiche and garnish with the parsley.

# Braised rabbit

**1.** Preheat the oven to 375°F (190°C).

**2.** Toss the rabbit joints in the flour until coated.

**3.** Heat the oil in a pan and cook the onion and garlic until soft. Stir in the cumin and thyme, and put into a large casserole dish.

**4.** Brown the rabbit joints in the pan until brown on all sides and put into the casserole dish. Season with salt and pepper.

**5.** Pour in the wine and stock, cover and cook for 1 hour.

**6.** Add the vegetables to the dish and continue cooking for a further hour until the rabbit is tender and the vegetables are cooked. Serve with polenta.

Preparation time: 20 min
Cooking time: 2 h 25 min
Serves 4

*6–8 rabbit joints*
*2 tbsp flour*
*4 tbsp oil*
*1 onion, chopped*
*2 garlic cloves, finely chopped*
*½ tsp ground cumin*
*2 tbsp chopped thyme*
*250ml dry white wine*
*250ml vegetable stock*
*200g carrots, sliced*
*150g French beans, halved*
*400g waxy potatoes, roughly chopped*

# Lentil, chorizo and root vegetable stew

**1.** Preheat the oven to 375°F (190°C).

**2.** Heat the oil in a flameproof casserole dish and fry the onion and garlic for 3–4 minutes until soft.

**3.** Add the potatoes, carrots, parsnips and red pepper, and cook for 6–7 minutes, until the vegetables are golden.

**4.** Stir in the curry powder, pour in the stock and bring to a boil. Add the lentils and chorizo, cover and cook in the oven for 20–30 minutes until the lentils and vegetables are tender and the sauce has thickened.

**5.** Garnish with sage leaves.

Preparation time: 20 min
Cooking time: 1 h
Serves 4

*2 tbsp oil*
*1 onion, chopped*
*2 garlic cloves, crushed*
*700g potatoes, peeled and cut into*
  *chunks*
*4 carrots, thickly sliced*
*2 parsnips, thickly sliced*
*1 red pepper, sliced*
*3 tomatoes, sliced*
*2 tbsp curry powder*
*1 litre vegetable stock*
*100g red lentils*
*175g chorizo, sliced*
*sage leaves, to serve*

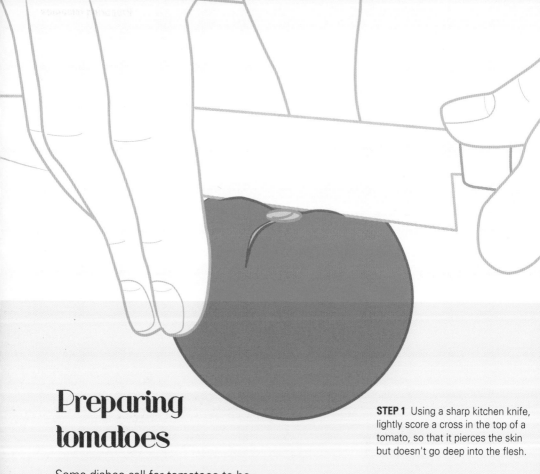

# Preparing tomatoes

Some dishes call for tomatoes to be used without skin or seeds, to give the finished dish a cleaner texture. This clever technique makes this a quick and easy job.

**STEP 1** Using a sharp kitchen knife, lightly score a cross in the top of a tomato, so that it pierces the skin but doesn't go deep into the flesh.

**STEP 2** Lower the scored tomato into a pan of boiling water using a slotted spoon. Cook for about 20 seconds or until the skin starts to split.

**STEP 3** Lift the tomato out of the water using a slotted spoon and plunge into iced water. When cool, pare away the skin with a small knife.

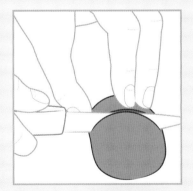

**STEP 4** When completely skinned, slice the tomato in half.

**STEP 5** Cut the tomato half into quarters then cut away the seeds.

# Lamb and pumpkin stew with peppers and red onions

**1.** Preheat the oven to 300°F (150°C).

**2.** Add salt and pepper to the flour and coat the pieces of lamb evenly.

**3.** Heat 1 tablespoon oil in a flameproof casserole dish and brown the lamb in batches. Remove from the dish and set aside.

**4.** Heat the remaining oil and cook the vegetables until soft. Add the lamb, rosemary leaves and the stock.

**5.** Cover and cook for 1–1½ hours until the meat and vegetables are tender.

Preparation time: 20 min
Cooking time: 1 h 45 min
Serves 4

*700g lamb, cubed*
*2 tbsp flour*
*2 tbsp oil*
*2 red onions, quartered*
*2 garlic cloves, crushed*
*500g pumpkin flesh, thickly sliced*
*2 red peppers, roughly chopped*
*1 rosemary sprig*
*250ml lamb stock*

# Cassoulet

**1.** Heat the oven to 300°F (150°C).

**2.** Drain the beans and place in a pan of fresh cold water, then bring to a boil and cook for 5 minutes. Drain well.

**3.** Tip the beans into a large pan. Add the diced pork rind and bacon and cover with fresh cold water. Bring to a boil and cook for 10 minutes. Drain the beans, rind and bacon.

**4.** Heat the goose fat or olive oil in a large flameproof casserole dish and fry the onion and garlic for 5 minutes. Add the thyme, cloves and bay leaves and continue cooking slowly for another 5 minutes. Add the sausage and cook until lightly browned.

**5.** Remove as much fat as possible from the confit goose and add the goose pieces to the pan with the blanched beans, diced pork rind and bacon. Pour in enough water to cover all the ingredients, then bring to a boil and skim off the scum. Season to taste with salt and pepper.

**6.** Cook uncovered in the oven for 2–4 hours, stirring occasionally. When the cassoulet is cooked, the beans will be soft and creamy in texture and the juices will have thickened. The actual cooking time depends on the beans you've used and your oven. If the cassoulet looks as if it's drying out during cooking, add more water.

**7.** Garnish with lettuce leaves.

Preparation time: 35 min
Cooking time: 4 h 20 min
Serves 4

500g haricot beans, soaked
    overnight in water
75g pork rind, diced
125g smoked streaky bacon, diced
2 tbsp goose fat or olive oil
1 onion, roughly chopped
2 garlic cloves
2 sprigs thyme
1 pinch ground cloves
2 bay leaves
350g garlic sausage, thickly sliced
350g goose confit
lettuce leaves, to garnish

# Chilli and cheese casserole

**1.** Heat the oil in a flameproof casserole dish and cook the onion, celery and chilli until soft. Season with salt and pepper. Remove the vegetables and set aside.

**2.** Brown the minced beef in the dish, then add the vegetables, chilli powder, tomatoes, tomato purée, beans and stock. Bring to a boil and simmer for 15 minutes.

**3.** Heat the oven to 400°F (200°C).

**4.** Cook the pasta according to the pack instructions. Drain and stir into the minced beef mixture.

**5.** Mix the yoghurt, eggs and cheese, and season lightly. Spoon the mixture over the casserole and bake for 20–25 minutes, until lightly browned.

**6.** Garnish with coriander and chillies.

Preparation time: 20 min
Cooking time: 55 min
Serves 4

*2 tbsp oil*
*1 large onion, chopped*
*2 sticks celery, chopped*
*1 red chilli, finely chopped*
*500g minced beef*
*2 tsp chilli powder*
*410g canned chopped tomatoes*
*1 tbsp tomato purée*
*400g canned kidney beans, drained*
*300ml beef stock*
*300g pasta*
*300ml plain yoghurt*
*2 eggs, beaten*
*110g grated cheese*
*coriander leaves, 1 red and 1 green*
  *chilli, to garnish*

# Cod and vegetable stew

Preparation time: 25 min
Cooking time: 1 h
Serves 4

*500g cod fillet, cut into chunks*
*1 lemon, juice*
*4 tbsp olive oil*
*1 onion, chopped*
*2 garlic cloves, crushed*
*1 red pepper, cut into strips*
*1 yellow pepper, cut into strips*
*200g pumpkin, roughly chopped*
*300ml fish stock*
*4cm piece ginger, finely chopped*
*200g canned sweetcorn, drained*
*200g peas*
*100ml boiling water*
*4 sprigs thyme*

**1.** Preheat the oven to 375°F (190°C).

**2.** Sprinkle salt, pepper and lemon juice over the chunks of fish.

**3.** Heat the oil in a flameproof casserole dish and cook the onion, garlic, peppers and pumpkin until just softened.

**4.** Add the stock, ginger, sweetcorn, peas, boiling water and the leaves from the thyme sprigs. Season to taste with salt and pepper.

**5.** Place the fish on top of the casserole. Cover and cook in the oven for 20–30 minutes, until the fish is cooked.

# Zucchini and tomato provencal

**1.** Preheat the oven to 350°F (180°C). Grease a baking dish.

**2.** Heat the olive oil in a large frying pan and fry the onion and garlic for 5 minutes until soft.

**3.** Add the courgettes and fry for 5 minutes until soft, then stir in the thyme and season with salt and pepper.

**4.** Add the courgettes into the baking dish and place the tomatoes on top. Sprinkle with the cheese.

**5.** Bake for 20–30 minutes until the cheese has melted.

Preparation time: 15 min
Cooking time: 40 min
Serves 4

*4 tbsp olive oil*
*2 onions, chopped*
*2 garlic cloves, crushed*
*450g courgettes, chopped*
*450g tomatoes, sliced*
*1 tbsp chopped thyme*
*110g grated cheese*

# Chicken casserole with pastry crust

**1**. Preheat the oven to 375°F (190°C).

**2**. Heat the oil in a flameproof casserole and quickly cook the chicken for a few minutes until golden brown. Remove from the dish and set aside.

**3**. Add the vegetables to the dish and cook for 3–5 minutes until just softened. Stir in the soup, milk and tarragon. Add the chicken and season to taste.

**4**. Roll out the pastry and cover the dish. Cook for about 30 minutes until the pastry is golden and the filling is piping hot.

Preparation time: 20 min
Cooking time: 50 min
Serves 4

2 tbsp oil
4 chicken breasts, roughly chopped
2 carrots, diced
1 onion, chopped
200g peas
1 can condensed chicken soup
milk (about two-thirds of the soup
   can)
½ tbsp chopped tarragon
225g shortcrust pastry

# Green bean casserole

**1.** Preheat the oven to 350°F (180°C). Butter a baking dish.

**2.** Melt the butter in a frying pan. Cook the onion, parsley and mushrooms until the onions are translucent and the mushrooms are giving off their juices.

**3.** Add the flour, salt, pepper and lemon juice. Cook until the flour is slightly browned.

**4.** Stir in the soured cream.

**5.** Cook the beans in a pan of salted boiling water for 5 minutes. Drain and stir into the mixture.

**6.** Pour the green bean mixture into the baking dish.

**7.** Mix together the cheese, breadcrumbs and melted butter and spread evenly over the top.

**8.** Bake for 20–30 minutes until it turns golden brown in colour.

Preparation time: 20 min
Cooking time: 50 min
Serves 4

*30 g butter*
*1 onion, diced*
*1 tbsp finely chopped parsley*
*100g mushrooms, diced*
*2 tbsp flour*
*1 tsp salt*
*½ tsp pepper*
*1 tsp lemon juice*
*250ml soured cream*
*400g French beans*
*110g grated Cheddar cheese*
*225g breadcrumbs*
*4 tbsp melted butter*

# Sweet potato casserole

Preparation time: 20 min
Cooking time: 50 min
Serves 4

*1kg sweet potatoes, peeled and*
*thinly sliced*
*2 tbsp olive oil*
*2 garlic cloves, finely chopped*
*1 tsp dried chilli flakes*
*250ml double cream*
*chopped chives, to serve*

*For the topping:*
*110g butter, melted*
*225g breadcrumbs*

**1.** Preheat the oven to 375°F (190°C). Grease a baking dish.

**2.** Mix all the ingredients together until the sweet potato slices are well coated. Place into the baking dish.

**3.** For the topping: mix the butter and breadcrumbs and season with salt and pepper.

**4.** Sprinkle over the sweet potatoes and bake for 40–50 minutes, until the topping is golden and crisp. Garnish with the chopped chives.

# Cauliflower stew with watercress

**1.** Preheat the oven to 375°F (190°C).

**2.** Heat the butter in a flameproof casserole dish. Cook the vegetables, except for the tomatoes, until softened.

**3.** Add the flour and cook for 1 minute. Cover and cook in the oven for 15 minutes.

**4.** Add the tomatoes, cream, stock and ham. Season with salt and pepper. Cook for a further 20 minutes.

**5.** Add the watercress just before serving.

Preparation time: 15 min
Cooking time: 40 min
Serves 4

*2 tbsp butter*
*1 cauliflower, divided into florets*
*1 onion, chopped*
*3 sticks celery, chopped*
*1 sweet potato, diced*
*2 tbsp flour*
*2 tomatoes, skinned and cut*
  *into strips*
*200ml double cream*
*500ml vegetable stock*
*100g cooked ham, diced*
*1 handful watercress*

# Ravioli casserole

**1.** For the pasta: flour a work surface and place the flour, eggs, egg yolk, oil and salt in the centre. Mix with your hands until you form a smooth dough. If necessary add some water. Wrap in cling film and chill for 1 hour.

**2.** Preheat the oven to 400°F (200°C). Butter a large baking dish.

**3.** For the filling: mix all the ingredients together.

**4.** Roll out the dough thinly on a floured work surface and cut in half to form 2 sheets of dough. Place 1 teaspoon of the filling at a distance of about 4 cm on 1 sheet of dough. Place the second sheet of dough on top and press down around the filling.

**5.** Chop the dough into small squares or rounds. Press the edges firmly together. Cook in a pan of boiling salted water for 1–2 minutes. Drain well.

**6.** Heat the butter in a frying pan and cook the garlic until just softened. Add the spinach and cook until wilted. Drain well. Whisk the eggs with the cream, crème fraîche and cheese. Season with salt and nutmeg.

**7.** Layer the ravioli with the tomatoes and spinach alternately in the baking dish and pour the cream mixture over each layer, ending with the cream mixture.

**8.** Cook for about 30 minutes until it turns golden brown in colour.

Preparation time: 30 min
  plus 1 h chilling
Cooking time: 50 min
Serves 4

*For the pasta:*
*300g plain flour*
*2 eggs, whisked*
*1 egg yolk*
*1 tbsp oil*
*1 pinch salt*

*For the filling:*
*250g ricotta cheese*
*grated nutmeg*
*4 tbsp grated Parmesan cheese*
*1 tbsp breadcrumbs*
*1 egg*

*To finish:*
*1 tbsp butter*
*1 garlic clove, finely chopped*
*1 handful spinach*
*2 eggs*
*250ml double cream*
*250ml crème fraîche*
*60g grated cheese*
*grated nutmeg*
*3 tomatoes, chopped*

# Seared sea bass with fava bean and arugula stew

**1.** Preheat the oven to 375°F (190°C).

**2.** Place all the ingredients, except the fish and oil, into a flameproof casserole dish. Bring to a boil.

**3.** Cover and cook in the oven for 1–1 ¼ hours, until the vegetables are tender.

**4.** Lightly score the skin of the fish and season with salt and freshly ground black pepper. Heat the oil in a frying pan and quickly fry the fish for about 1–2 minutes on each side, until cooked through.

**5.** For the garnish: heat the olive oil in a frying pan and fry the bread until crisp and golden. Chop into cubes.

**6.** Place the fish on top of the casserole and garnish with the fried bread and rocket.

Preparation time: 20 min
Cooking time: 1 h 25 min
Serves 4

*1kg broad beans*
*300g tomatoes, diced*
*2 sticks celery, chopped*
*1 can kidney beans, drained*
*2 garlic cloves, finely chopped*
*1 thyme sprig*
*½ tsp salt*
*4 sea bass fillets*
*1 tbsp oil*

*To serve:*
*4 tbsp olive oil*
*5 slices bread*
*rocket leaves, torn*

# Baked spinach dip

**1.** Heat the oven to 400°F (200°C). Grease a baking dish.

**2.** Cook the macaroni according to the pack instructions. Drain well and put into the baking dish. Sprinkle over the ham.

**3.** Heat the oil in a frying pan and cook the onion and garlic until soft. Add the spinach and cook until just wilted. Tip into the baking dish.

**4.** Sprinkle over half the grated cheese.

**5.** Melt the butter in a pan and stir in the flour. Cook for 1 minute until it forms a smooth paste. Remove from the flame and whisk in the cream, milk and soft cheese.

**6.** Bring to a boil, whisking, and stir in the remaining grated cheese. Season with salt and pepper.

**7.** Pour into the baking dish and stir well. Bake for 40–60 minutes until lightly browned and bubbling. Let it stand for 10 minutes before serving.

Preparation time: 15 min
Cooking time: 1 h 10 min
Serves 4

*300g macaroni*
*200g cooked ham, chopped*
*oil*
*1 onion, finely chopped*
*2 garlic cloves, finely chopped*
*450g spinach, chopped*
*300g grated cheese*
*50g butter*
*50g flour*
*150ml double cream*
*500ml milk*
*3 tbsp soft cheese*

# Lamb and dandelion casserole

**1.** Heat the oven to 350°F (180°C).

**2.** Heat the oil in a flameproof casserole dish and brown the lamb in batches.

**3.** Add the onions to the dish and cook until just softened. Pour in the passata and water and season with salt and pepper. Add the dandelion leaves.

**4.** Cover and cook for 1 ¼ hours until the meat is tender. Add the tomatoes and cook for a further 15 minutes.

**5.** Cook the potatoes in boiling salted water for about 20 minutes, until tender. Drain and mash with the hot milk and season to taste with nutmeg, salt and pepper.

**6.** Spread on top of the casserole and sprinkle with grated cheese. Cook for a further 20 minutes until the potatoes are golden and the cheese has melted. Garnish with rosemary.

Preparation time: 20 min
Cooking time: 2 h 20 min
Serves 4

*2 tbsp oil*
*1kg boneless lamb shoulder, cubed*
*2 onions, chopped*
*200ml passata*
*200ml water*
*450g dandelion leaves*
*6 tomatoes, quartered*
*450g potatoes, peeled and cut into*
  *chunks*
*40ml hot milk*
*grated nutmeg*
*50g Cheddar cheese, grated*
*rosemary sprigs, to serve*

# Broccoli rice casserole

Preparation time: 20 min
Cooking time: 40 min
Serves 4

*1 onion, chopped*
*250g broccoli, stalks chopped and*
*    florets halved*
*400ml vegetable stock*
*1 tsp French mustard*
*200ml crème fraîche*
*225g grated Gruyère cheese*
*550g cooked long-grain white*
*    rice, cooled*
*½ teaspoon salt*
*1 large egg*

**1.** Heat the oven to 375°F (190°C). Butter a baking dish.

**2.** Cook the onion and broccoli stalks in a pan of lightly salted boiling water for 7 minutes. Add the florets and cook for another 3 minutes.

**3.** Whisk together the stock, mustard and crème fraîche and season to taste with salt and pepper. Bring to a boil. Stir in the vegetables and half the cheese, mixing until melted. Transfer to the baking dish.

**4.** Mix together the rice, salt, egg and the remaining cheese. Spread on top of the baking dish.

**5.** Cook for 20–30 minutes until the topping is crisp and golden.

# Pinto bean stew

**1**. Heat the oven to 375°F (190°C).

**2**. Drain the beans and place in a large pan. Pour in some fresh water. Bring to a boil and cook for 10 minutes. Drain and set aside.

**3**. Heat the oil in a flameproof casserole dish and cook the onion, carrots and garlic until softened. Stir in the cumin, beans and passata. Season to taste with salt, pepper and cayenne.

**4**. Cover and cook in the oven for 1–1 ½ hours until the beans are tender. Garnish with chopped coriander.

Preparation time: 15 min
Cooking time: 1 h 50 min
Serves 4

*600g dried pinto beans, soaked in
    water overnight*
*1 tbsp olive oil*
*1 onion, diced*
*2 carrots, diced*
*2 garlic cloves, crushed*
*1 tsp ground cumin*
*1 x 600g jar passata*
*1 pinch cayenne pepper*
*chopped coriander, to serve*

# Lamb and fennel

**1.** Heat the oven to 325°F (160°C).

**2.** Heat the oil in a flameproof casserole dish and brown the meat. Season with salt and pepper and add the vegetables. Cook until golden.

**3.** Stir in the lemon juice, chopped fennel, stock and wine and bring to a boil.

**4.** Cover and cook in the oven for 50–60 minutes, until the meat and vegetables are tender.

Preparation time: 15 min
Cooking time: 1 h 15 min
Serves 4

*3 tbsp olive oil*
*1kg stewing lamb, cubed*
*1 onion, chopped*
*2 garlic cloves, finely chopped*
*3 large fennel bulbs, quartered*
*juice of 1 lemon*
*2 tbsp chopped fennel*
*200ml lamb stock*
*100ml dry white wine*

# White bean, carrot and cabbage stew

**1.** Heat the oven to 375°F (190°C).

**2.** Bring the stock to a boil in a flameproof casserole dish. Add the carrots and cabbage. Cook for 8–10 minutes, until tender.

**3.** Stir in the olive oil, cream, beans and thyme and season to taste with salt and pepper.

**4.** Mix the breadcrumbs and butter and season to taste. Spoon on top of the vegetables.

**5.** Cover and cook in the oven for about 20 minutes until the topping is crisp and golden.

Preparation time: 15 min
Cooking time: 35 min
Serves 4

*500ml vegetable stock*
*3 carrots, sliced*
*¼ cabbage, shredded*
*1 tbsp olive oil*
*3 tbsp double cream*
*2 x 400g cans white beans, drained*
*1 tbsp chopped thyme*
*110g breadcrumbs*
*50g melted butter*

# Moroccan chickpea stew

Preparation time: 15 min
Cooking time: 1 h 20 min
Serves 4

*3 tbsp olive oil*
*1 onion, chopped*
*1 garlic clove, crushed*
*2 tsp ground cumin*
*4 cinnamon sticks, broken into*
  *pieces*
*175g canned chickpeas, drained*
*500g pumpkin flesh, chopped into*
  *large chunks*
*4 waxy potatoes, chopped into*
  *large chunks*
*200g canned chopped tomatoes*
*1 preserved lemon, roughly*
  *chopped*
*110g green olives*

**1.** Preheat the oven to 350°F (180°C).

**2.** Heat the oil in a flameproof casserole dish. Cook the onion and garlic for 3 minutes, until soft.

**3.** Add the cumin and cinnamon sticks and cook for a further 2 minutes. Add the chickpeas, pumpkin, potatoes and tomatoes. Pour in water, if needed, to cover.

**4.** Season with salt and pepper to taste. Cover and cook in the oven for about 1 hour, until the pumpkin is tender. Add the preserved lemon and olives and cook for a further 10 minutes.

# Shellfish cioppino

**1.** Heat 2 tablespoons oil in a large pan and cook the garlic and shallots until they turn golden brown in colour.

**2.** Add the stock, passata, chilli flakes, Tabasco sauce and wine and bring to a boil. Simmer for 15 minutes.

**3.** Heat the remaining oil in a frying pan and cook the snapper until golden brown on both sides.

**4.** Add the shrimps, mussels, clams and squid to the large pan. Cook until the clams and mussels open (throw away any that remain closed). Add the cooked rice and peas and season to taste.

**5.** Place the snapper in a serving dish and add the shellfish stew on top. Sprinkle with herbs and garnish with the cooked lobster.

Preparation time: 15 min
Cooking time: 40 min
Serves 4

*4 tbsp olive oil*
*1 garlic clove, crushed*
*2 shallots, chopped*
*300ml fish stock*
*90ml tomato passata*
*¼ tsp chilli flakes*
*¼ tsp Tabasco sauce*
*100ml white wine*
*350g red snapper fillets*
*12 large raw shrimps, de-veined*
*600ml mussels*
*600ml clams*
*150g small squid, chopped into pieces*
*120g cooked rice*
*100g peas*
*1 tbsp chopped fresh herbs, parsley, chervil and basil*
*1 cooked lobster*

# Hunter's stew with venison, lentils and mushroom

**1.** Preheat the oven to 300°F (150°C).

**2.** Toss the meat in the flour, salt and pepper.

**3.** Heat the oil in a flameproof casserole dish and brown the meat in batches. Remove the meat and set aside.

**4.** Add the onions and carrots to the casserole dish and cook for 5 minutes or until light golden brown. Add the venison to the dish with the bay leaves and lentils.

**5.** Add the wine and stock and bring to a boil. Cover and cook in the oven for 2–2 ½ hours until the meat is tender.

**6.** Heat the butter in a frying pan and cook the mushrooms until golden. Place on top of the casserole and garnish with rosemary.

Preparation time: 20 min
Cooking time: 2 h 45 min
Serves 4

*1.3kg venison, cubed*
*3 tbsp flour*
*1 tbsp oil*
*2 onions, chopped*
*2 carrots, chopped*
*2 bay leaves*
*145g red lentils*
*150ml dry red wine*
*1 litre game stock*
*2 tbsp butter*
*175g wild or button mushrooms*
*rosemary sprigs, to serve*

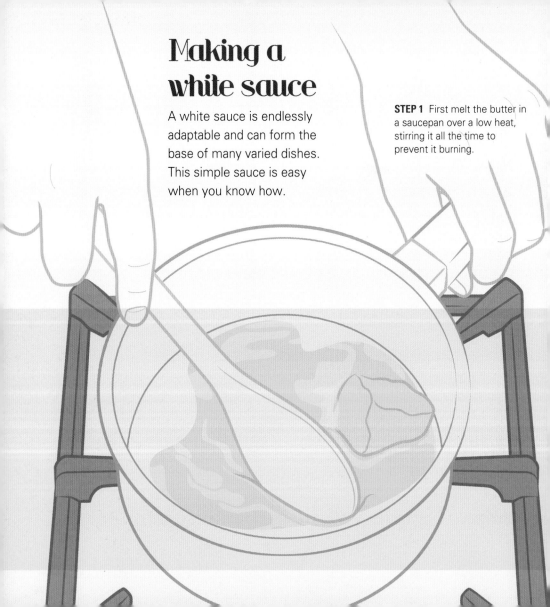

# Making a white sauce

A white sauce is endlessly adaptable and can form the base of many varied dishes. This simple sauce is easy when you know how.

**STEP 1** First melt the butter in a saucepan over a low heat, stirring it all the time to prevent it burning.

**STEP 2** When all the butter is melted, tip in the flour, stirring all the time.

**STEP 3** Cook for about a minute, stirring, until it is pale yellow.

**STEP 4** Slowly add the liquid, pouring in a little at a time and mixing it in. Use a whisk to beat out lumps.

**STEP 5** For a cheese sauce, add some grated cheese to the mixture. Cook until melted and stir in until smooth.

# Whole guinea-fowl

**1.** Preheat the oven to 400°F (200°C).

**2.** Heat the butter in a flameproof casserole dish. Cook the onion and pepper until just softened.

**3.** Add the bay leaves and thyme and pour in the stock and cranberry sauce. Bring to a boil, then remove from the flame. Season to taste with salt and pepper. Place the guinea fowl on top of the vegetables.

**4.** Cover and cook in the oven for 45 minutes. Remove the cover and continue cooking for a further 15–25 minutes (depending on the size of the bird) until the guinea fowl is tender and cooked.

Preparation time: 15 min
Cooking time: 1 h 20 min
Serves 2–4

*50g butter*
*1 onion, diced*
*1 red pepper, sliced*
*2 bay leaves*
*1 pinch dried thyme*
*450ml chicken stock*
*2 tsp cranberry sauce*
*1 guinea fowl*

# Jerusalem artichoke casserole

**1.** Preheat the oven to 375°F (190°C). Butter a baking dish.

**2.** Heat the butter in a pan and gently cook the leeks until softened.

**3.** Layer the leek and onion mixture with the artichokes and celeriac in the baking dish, seasoning as you go.

**4.** Mix together the crème fraîche and stock and pour into the dish. Cover with foil and bake for 30 minutes or until the vegetables are nearly tender. Remove the foil, scatter over the cheese and bake for a further 15–20 minutes.

Preparation time: 15 min
Cooking time: 1 h
Serves 4

*2 tbsp butter*
*1 leek, white part only; chopped*
*1 onion, chopped*
*450g Jerusalem artichokes, scrubbed and chopped in half*
*200g celeriac, peeled and roughly chopped*
*250g crème fraîche*
*150ml vegetable stock*
*150g Emmental cheese, grated*

# Veal tagine with almonds

**1.** Preheat the oven to 300°F (150°C).

**2.** Mix together the cayenne, black pepper, paprika, ginger, turmeric and cinnamon. Toss the veal in half of the spice mix. Cover and leave overnight in the refrigerator.

**3.** Heat 2 tablespoons olive oil in a frying pan and 1 tablespoon oil in a large flameproof casserole dish. Add the onions and remaining spice mix to the pan and cook slowly for 10 minutes until the onions are soft, but not browned. Add the crushed garlic for the final 3 minutes.

**4.** In a separate frying pan, heat the remaining oil and brown the veal cubes on all sides. Add the browned meat to the casserole dish.

**5.** Deglaze the frying pan with 150 ml tomato juice and add these juices to the pan.

**6.** Add the remaining tomato juice, chopped tomatoes, apricots, prunes, raisins, almonds, saffron, stock and honey to the casserole dish. Bring to a boil, cover and cook in the oven for 2–2 ½ hours, until the meat is tender.

**7.** Sprinkle with sesame seeds just before serving.

Preparation time: 20 min
Cooking time: 2 h 50 min
Serves 4

*1 tsp cayenne pepper*
*2 tsp ground black pepper*
*1 tbsp paprika*
*1 tbsp ground ginger*
*1 tbsp turmeric*
*2 tsp ground cinnamon*
*1kg veal, cut into 5 cm cubes*
*2 large onions, finely chopped*
*4 tbsp olive oil*
*3 garlic cloves, crushed*
*600ml tomato juice*
*2 x 400g canned chopped tomatoes*
*110g dried apricots, halved*
*110g prunes*
*50g raisins*
*85g blanched almonds, toasted*
*1 tsp saffron*
*600ml veal stock*
*1 tbsp honey*

# Vegetarian chilli

Preparation time: 15 min
Cooking time: 1 h
Serves 4

*2 tbsp oil*
*1 large onion, chopped*
*2 garlic cloves, crushed*
*1–2 tsp chilli powder*
*1 tsp ground cumin*
*1 red pepper, chopped*
*1 green pepper, chopped*
*1 yellow pepper, chopped*
*2 x 400 g cans chopped tomatoes*
*1 tbsp tomato purée*
*300ml vegetable stock*
*1 can kidney beans, drained*
*soured cream and ground*
  *cinnamon, to serve*

**1.** Preheat the oven to 375°F (190°C).

**2.** Heat the oil in a flameproof casserole dish. Fry the onion and garlic together with the chilli and cumin, until the onions are softening.

**3.** Add the peppers and cook for 5 minutes, stirring all the time. Add the tomatoes, purée and stock and bring to a boil. Season to taste with salt and pepper.

**4.** Cover and cook in the oven for 30–35 minutes until piping hot. Add the kidney beans for the last 10 minutes of the cooking time.

**5.** Garnish with soured cream sprinkled with cinnamon.

# Potato casserole with tomatoes and onions

**1.** Preheat the oven to 375°F (190°C).

**2.** Place the potatoes in a pan with water to cover. Bring to a boil and simmer for 3 minutes. Drain well.

**3.** Brush 1 tablespoon of oil over the base and sides of a baking dish. Layer the potatoes, tomatoes, onion and rosemary in the dish, seasoning and drizzling each layer with oil.

**4.** Bake for 45–55 minutes, until the top is lightly browned.

Preparation time: 20 min
Cooking time: 1 h 30 min
Serves 4

*750g potatoes, peeled and thinly*
 *sliced*
*4–5 tbsp olive oil*
*750g tomatoes, sliced*
*1 onion, sliced*
*1 tbsp chopped rosemary*

# Wild rabbit with mushrooms and medlars

**1.** Marinate the rabbit in the olive oil, garlic and rice wine for at least 2 hours.

**2.** Preheat the oven to 375°F (190°C).

**3.** Heat the oil in a flameproof casserole dish and brown the rabbit joints until brown on all sides. Add the carrots, drained mushrooms, onion and garlic and cook for 3 minutes.

**4.** Add the reserved marinade, salt and pepper and pour in the wine, stock and soy sauce. Season with salt and pepper to taste.

**5.** Add the medlars and cover and cook for 1–1 ½ hours until the rabbit is tender.

Preparation time: 20 min
plus 2 h marinating
Cooking time: 2 h
Serves 4

*6–8 rabbit joints*
*2 tbsp olive oil*
*1 garlic clove, chopped*
*1 tbsp rice wine*
*2 tbsp oil*
*250g baby carrots*
*20g Chinese mushrooms, soaked in warm water for 20 minutes*
*1 onion, chopped*
*2 garlic cloves, finely chopped*
*250ml dry white wine*
*250ml vegetable stock*
*2 tbsp soy sauce*
*200g bletted medlars*

# Vegetable stew with lobster

**1.** Preheat the oven to 375°F (190°C).

**2.** Heat the butter in a flameproof casserole dish and cook the mushrooms until they are golden brown in colour.

**3.** Stir in the remaining ingredients except for the lobster and heat until very hot.

**4.** Cover and cook in the oven for 15–20 minutes until heated through.

**5.** Place the lobster on top of the casserole and sprinkle with the chopped chives.

Preparation time: 20 min
Cooking time: 35 min
Serves 4

*2 tbsp butter*
*175g button mushrooms, sliced*
*2 tbsp flour*
*300ml vegetable stock*
*100ml plain yoghurt*
*1 pinch grated nutmeg*
*300g white asparagus tips*
*300g sweetcorn, drained*
*400g canned white beans, drained*
*450g cooked lobster meat*
*chopped chives, to serve*

# Lamb tagine

Preparation time: 15 min
Cooking time: 2 h 45 min
Serves 4

*2 tbsp oil*
*4 lamb shanks*
*2 onions, sliced*
*2 garlic cloves, crushed*
*1 tsp ground cinnamon*
*1 tsp ground cumin*
*1 tsp ground ginger*
*1 tsp turmeric*
*10 dates, halved*
*1 x 400 g can chopped tomatoes*
*lamb stock*
*thyme sprigs, to serve*

**1.** Preheat the oven to 300°F (150°C).

**2.** Heat the oil in a frying pan and brown the lamb shanks on all sides.

**3.** Place into a large casserole dish with the onions, garlic, spices, dates, tomatoes and enough stock to just cover the meat.

**4.** Cover and cook for 2–2 ½ hours until the meat is tender. Garnish with thyme sprigs.

# Chicken stew with mushrooms and tarragon

**1.** Preheat the oven to 375°F (190°C).

**2.** Toss the chicken pieces in the flour, salt and pepper.

**3.** Heat the oil in a flameproof casserole dish. Add the chicken and onion and cook until the chicken is browned all over. Do this in batches if necessary.

**4.** Add the mushrooms and cook for a further 5 minutes. Add the potatoes and tarragon and pour in the stock. Bring to a boil.

**5.** Cover and cook in the oven for 45–60 minutes, until the chicken is cooked. Garnish with tarragon.

Preparation time: 15 min
Cooking time: 1 h 15 min
Serves 4

*4 chicken legs*
*2 tbsp flour*
*5 tbsp olive oil*
*1 onion, sliced*
*200g button mushrooms, sliced*
*8 small potatoes, peeled*
*1 tbsp chopped tarragon*
*400ml chicken stock*
*fresh tarragon, to serve*

# Savoy and carrot stew

**1.** Heat the butter in a large pan. Add the carrots and cook for 3–4 minutes.

**2.** Stir in the cabbage and cook for 2 minutes until wilted.

**3.** Pour over the stock and simmer for about 5 minutes, until the carrots are just cooked. Season to taste with salt and pepper.

Preparation time: 10 min
Cooking time: 15 min
Serves 4

*2 tbsp butter*
*2 carrots, chopped into small chunks*
*1 Savoy cabbage, cored and*
 *quartered*
*300ml vegetable stock*

# Making dumplings

Dumplings are the wonderfully satisfying finish to a warming, hearty casserole. These fluffy, doughy balls are easy to prepare and cook gently on top of the casserole.

**STEP 1** First chop all the herbs using a mezzaluna – rock it from side to side to finely chop – or a very sharp knife.

**STEP 2** Combine the flour and suet in a mixing bowl and season with salt and pepper. Mix in the chopped herbs.

**STEP 3** Pour in the water a little at a time and stir in to make a soft, pliable dough. Add more water if needed.

**STEP 4** Bring the mixture together into one large ball then divide into smaller pieces. Roll each into a small ball using floured hands.

**STEP 5** Using a slotted spoon, lower each dumpling into the casserole and cook, with the lid on, for the last 25 minutes of the dish's cooking time.

# Pot-roasted beef with shallots

**1.** Preheat the oven to 325°F (170°C). Heat the oil in a large casserole dish. Fry the beef on a high flame on all sides for about 4–5 minutes, until it turns golden brown in colour. Lift out of the pan and set aside.

**2.** Add the shallots to the dish and fry for 5 minutes, turning occasionally, until they turn golden in colour. Stir in the garlic and cook for 2 minutes. Stir in the herbs, wine, stock and purée until well blended.

**3.** Return the beef to the dish and bring to a boil. Cover and bake for 3–3 ½ hours, turning the beef occasionally during cooking. Remove the beef from the dish and place on a warmed serving plate. Cover and allow to rest for 30 minutes.

**4.** Discard any sprigs and bay leaves. Stir the honey into the dish juices. Garnish with fresh thyme.

Preparation time: 20 min
Cooking time: 3 h 45 min
 plus resting
Serves 4

*2 tbsp olive oil*
*1.4kg silverside of beef*
*22 shallots, peeled*
*4 garlic cloves, sliced*
*good bunch fresh thyme*
*2 sprigs rosemary*
*2 bay leaves*
*350ml red wine*
*300ml good beef stock*
*3 tbsp tomato purée*
*1 tbsp honey*
*fresh thyme, to garnish*

# Oxtail with Guinness

**1.** Preheat the oven to 325°F (170°C). Season the flour and then toss in the oxtail pieces to coat evenly. Heat 2 tablespoons of the oil in a large casserole dish. Fry the oxtail pieces, in batches, until they turn golden brown in colour. Lift out of the pan and set aside.

**2.** Heat the remaining oil and cook the bacon for 5 minutes, until golden. Using a slotted spoon remove the bacon from the casserole dish and set aside.

**3.** Add the onions, celery, carrots and garlic to the casserole and cook for 5 minutes, until softened. Return the bacon to the dish with the tomato puree, Guinness, stock and thyme. Return the oxtail to the dish and bring to the boil. Season, cover and bake for about 5–5 ½ hours or until oxtail is cooked.

**4.** Remove the dish from the oven and skim off any fat. Taste juices and stir in redcurrant jelly if required. Serve with mash and shredded cabbage.

Preparation time: 15 min
Cooking time: 6 h
Serves 6

*2½ tbsp plain flour*
*2 kg oxtail*
*4 tbsp olive oil*
*250g smoked streak bacon, chopped*
  *thickly*
*2 onions, thickly sliced*
*2 sticks celery, sliced*
*2 medium carrots, diced or sliced*
*2 garlic cloves, chopped*
*4 tbsp tomato purée*
*2 x 440ml cans Guinness*
*400ml good beef stock*
*few sprigs of thyme*
*1 tbsp redcurrant jelly (optional)*

# Baked bolognese sauce

**1.** Preheat the oven to 300°F (150°C). Heat a large ovenproof dish and fry the mince and bacon for about 8–10 minutes, stirring occasionally until browned. Break any lumps in the meat.

**2.** Add the onion, celery and carrots and cook for 5 minutes, stirring occasionally. Stir in the remaining ingredients, until well blended and bring to the boil. Cover and bake for 2 hours, stirring occasionally.

**3.** Remove from the heat and serve with pasta.

Preparation time: 20 min
Cooking time: 2 h 20 min
Serves 6

600g good minced beef
4 rashers smoked streaky bacon, chopped
1 large onion, chopped
2 sticks celery, sliced
2 medium carrots, diced
2 garlic cloves, chopped
1 tbsp paprika
1 tbsp dried mixed herbs
1 x 300g jars chopped tomatoes
200ml red wine
250ml good beef stock
1 tbsp redcurrant jelly

# Lancashire hotpot

Preparation time: 15 min
Cooking time: 2 h 40 min
Serves 4

*900g lamb shoulder blade, cut
  into large pieces*
*900g waxy potatoes*
*3 lambs kidneys, skinned, cored
  and sliced, optional*
*2 medium carrots, sliced*
*2 medium onions, sliced*
*2 sticks celery*
*2 tbsp fresh chopped thyme*
*1 bay leaf*
*300ml good lamb stock*
*25g butter, melted*

**1.** Preheat the oven to 350°F (180°C). Lightly grease a deep ovenproof casserole dish. Using a sharp knife, remove excess fat from the lamb. Slice potatoes 5-mm thick and arrange a layer of the potatoes on the base of the prepared casserole.

**2.** Layer the lamb chops, kidneys, carrots, onions and celery in the casserole sprinkling with thyme and seasoning between each layer. Add bay leaf and pour over the stock.

**3.** Arrange the remaining potatoes in overlapping layers on top. Brush with butter then cover and bake for 2 hours. Uncover and bake for a further 30–40 minutes, until potatoes are golden.

# Chicken veronique

**1.** Heat the butter and oil together in a casserole dish and fry the chicken legs for about 5–10 minutes, turning until they are browned all over. Transfer to a plate and keep warm. Drain off half the fat left in the pan.

**2.** Add the onion and cook for 5 minutes, until softened. Return the chicken to the pan and pour over the wine, stock and tarragon. Season and bring to the boil and cover and simmer for 25–30 minutes, until the chicken is tender.

**3.** Transfer the chicken a plate and keep warm. Blend 3 tablespoons of the pan juices with the cornflour and set aside. Bring the pan juices to the boil and boil rapidly until reduced by half.

**4.** Stir in the cream and bring back to the boil and simmer for 2–3 minutes, until thickened. Stir in cornflour mixture, bring back to the boil, stirring until thickened. Return the chicken and grapes and bring back to the boil. Serve on hot serving plates and scatter over fresh chopped tarragon.

Preparation time: 10 min
Cooking time: 1 h
Serves 4

*25g butter*
*1 tbsp olive oil*
*4 chicken legs*
*1 onion, sliced*
*300ml white wine*
*150ml good chicken stock*
*1–2 tbsp fresh chopped tarragon*
*1 tbsp cornflour*
*150ml double cream*
*125g seedless white grapes, halved*
*chopped fresh tarragon, to garnish*

# Spanish lentil stew

**1.** Heat the olive oil in a large pan and gently cook the onions and garlic until translucent. Add the chorizo and cook for 3 minutes.

**2.** Add the remaining ingredients, except for the potatoes. Cover with water and bring to a boil. Reduce the heat and simmer for 20 minutes.

**3.** Add the potatoes and simmer for a further 20 minutes. Season to taste with salt and cayenne pepper.

Preparation time: 50 min
Cooking time: 45 min
Serves 4

*80ml olive oil*
*1 onion, diced*
*2 cloves garlic, crushed*
*200g chorizo, sliced*
*230g brown lentils, soaked overnight*
*  and drained*
*3 carrots, sliced*
*1 green bell pepper, diced*
*1 tomato, diced*
*2 tsp ground paprika*
*1 bay leaf*
*200g potatoes, peeled and diced*
*salt and cayenne pepper, to taste*

# Bean stew with chorizo

**1.** Put the drained beans in a large pan with fresh water and bring to a boil. Boil briskly for 10 minutes and drain.

**2.** Heat the oil in a frying pan and fry the onion for 5 minutes until softened. Add the carrots, celery and garlic and cook for 2 minutes.

**3.** Add to the beans in the large pan, with the tomatoes, stock, wine, salt and pepper and bring to a boil.

**4.** Stir in the chorizo and bouquet garni.

**5.** Cover and simmer for about 1 hour, until the beans are tender.

Preparation time: 10 min
  plus 12 h soaking
Cooking time: 1 h 20 min
Serves 4

250g dried haricot beans, soaked
  overnight
2 tbsp oil
1 onion, chopped
2 carrots, diced
1 stick celery, diced
2 cloves garlic, finely chopped
400g canned tomatoes, chopped
200ml vegetable stock
100ml red wine
salt and pepper
150g chorizo sausage, thickly sliced
1 bouquet garni

# Courgette and potato bake with whole unpeeled tomatoes

Preparation time: 5 min
Cooking time: 45 min
Serves 4

250g boiled potatoes, sliced
2 courgettes, sliced
350ml double cream
grated nutmeg
½ tsp sugar
125g grated Gruyère cheese
18 small tomatoes
salt and pepper, to taste

To garnish:
1 tbsp chopped parsley

**1.** Heat the oven to (180°C). Grease a baking dish.

**2.** Layer two-thirds of the potatoes and courgettes in the baking dish.

**3.** Mix together the cream, salt, pepper, nutmeg and sugar. Pour half into the baking dish and sprinkle with half the cheese.

**4.** Arrange the whole tomatoes in the dish and place the remaining potato and courgette slices between the tomatoes.

**5.** Sprinkle with the remaining cheese and pour over the remaining cream mixture. Bake for about 30 minutes until golden brown and bubbling.

**6.** Garnish with chopped parsley.

# Chilli beef with winter vegetables

**1.** Heat the oil in a large pan and brown the meat on all sides.

**2.** Add the onions and garlic and fry briefly, then add the curry powder, cayenne pepper and cumin.

**3.** Add the stock, cover and simmer for 30 minutes.

**4.** Add the potatoes, tomatoes, chickpeas and peas and simmer gently for a further 40–50 minutes. Stir occasionally and add more stock if necessary.

**5.** Season to taste and serve scattered with pumpkin seeds.

Preparation time: 1 h 30 min
Cooking time: 45 min
Serves 4

*2 tbsp oil*
*600g stewing beef, cubed*
*2 onions, chopped*
*2 cloves garlic, chopped*
*1 pinch curry powder*
*1 pinch cayenne pepper*
*1 pinch ground cumin*
*400ml beef stock*
*600g baking potatoes, peeled and
    chopped*
*5 tomatoes, diced*
*200g canned chickpeas, drained*
*200g frozen peas*
*salt, to taste*

*To garnish:*
*2 tbsp pumpkin seeds, toasted*

# Summer vegetable bake

**1.** Heat the oven to 350°F (180°C). Butter a baking dish.

**2.** Heat the oil in a frying pan and quickly brown the courgettes. Remove and season with salt and pepper.

**3.** Add the onions to the pan and cook until softened.

**4.** Layer the tomatoes, courgettes and onions in the baking dish, crumbling in the Ricotta. Season to taste. Trickle with olive oil and scatter the cheese over the top. Add the sage leaves and bake for 20–25 minutes, until bubbling.

Preparation time: 40 min
Cooking time: 35 min
Serves 4

*2 tbsp oil*
*500g courgettes, sliced*
*salt and pepper*
*1 onion, chopped*
*750g tomatoes, quartered*
*250g Ricotta*
*2–3 tsp olive oil*
*250g grated Cheddar cheese*
*sage leaves*

# Index

Notes

Notes

Notes

# Notes

# Favourite recipes

# Favourite recipes

# Favourite recipes

# Favourite recipes

# Favourite recipes

# Favourite recipes

# Favourite recipes